THE PROGRESSIVE PRESIDENTS

By the same author:

Joe Tumulty and the Wilson Era
The Republican Roosevelt
Woodrow Wilson and the Politics of Morality
The Promise of America
Roosevelt and Morgenthau
V Was for Victory
Years of Discord: American Politics and
Society, 1961–1974

THE
PROGRESSIVE
PRESIDENTS

Roosevelt, Wilson, Roosevelt, Johnson

John Morton Blum

W. W. NORTON & COMPANY

New York   London

First published as a Norton paperback 1982

Copyright © 1980 by W.W. Norton & Company, Inc.

Printed in the United States of America.

Library of Congress Cataloging in Publication Data
Blum, John Morton, 1921–
    The progressive Presidents—Roosevelt, Wilson,
Roosevelt, Johnson.
    Bibliography: p.
    Includes index.
    1. United States—Politics and government—20th
century.   2. Executive power—United States.
I. Title.
E743.B613   1980   353.03′2   79–22866

ISBN 0-393-00063-X

W. W. Norton & Company, Inc., 500 Fifth Avenue, New York, NY 10110
W. W. Norton & Company Ltd, 10 Coptic Street, London WC1A 1PU
    4 5 6 7 8 9 0

For Mary Louise and Kingman Brewster

Contents

Preface

THIS BOOK approaches a subject which has been troubling historians for the last dozen years and more. Those of us—"conventional liberals" in the pejorative phrase of both our conservative and our radical critics—who grew up during the administrations of Franklin D. Roosevelt and admired him, believed, as he did, in a strong presidency as an instrument of social and economic reform and of sensitive and intelligent foreign policy. We found in the administrations of Theodore Roosevelt and Woodrow Wilson some significant precedents on which Franklin Roosevelt built, and we regularly rated the three progressive presidents high on any list of all previous chief executives. Accordingly we were also on the whole skeptical about the relatively narrow view of the presidency shared in this century by William Howard Taft, Herbert C. Hoover, and Dwight D. Eisenhower.

Generally we had therefore substantial hopes for John F. Kennedy and, after his assassination, for Lyndon B. Johnson who seemed for several years to be operating within the tradition of his progressive predecessors. By 1967 those hopes and that appearance had largely evaporated. A developing anxiety about an "Imperial Presidency" provoked a reconsideration of the progressive presidents even before the excesses of Richard Nixon, from whom liberals had never expected anything admirable. That reconsideration drew in part from important criticisms from the left about the origins and effects of progressive policies of gradualistic reforms. Conservatives had long been asking similar questions for which they often provided a similar answer about the presidency. Like the radicals, they urged diminishing that office.

More recent experiences with episodes of presidential indecision or inaction suggest that Congress and the courts cannot rule alone. The presidency, though properly less exalted than some of its incumbents have tried to make it, has exerted in several productive reasons an effective force for social action. Presidential leadership need not be imperial; presidential lassitude has ordinarily been enervating for American politics and government. This book ventures another reassessment—here of the progressive presidents, their accomplishments, their legacy and Lyndon Johnson's confusing relationship to it—a reassessment of necessity inconclusive, but perhaps cautiously encouraging at least for liberals who have begun to emerge from their recent crises of belief.

JOHN MORTON BLUM
New Haven, Connecticut

Prologue: Ascutney

ON MT. ASCUTNEY, Vermont, shortly before noon on a late August Saturday in 1967, a day barely touched by the imminence of autumn, there began to gather several thousand men and women, local Vermont and New Hampshire farmers and merchants and mechanics; summer folk—lawyers, doctors, executives—from New York and Massachusetts, more by at least twice than the ski lodge kitchen had expected to provide with luncheon. Those who had brought their own sandwiches shared them with hungry strangers and their children. The growing picnic spread beyond the grounds of the lodge, across the tops of the ski slopes, naked in the summer sunlight and damp from the morning's drizzle, now spent. Yet the occasion was not festive. The picnickers had come to hear a serious speech critical of the American war in Vietnam, and to participate in one of a half-dozen workshops scheduled to follow that speech and to discuss related topics. As it developed before the afternoon was over, those workshops, each designed to accommodate perhaps twenty people, attracted on the average a hundred or even a hundred and fifty. They ran on until early evening when the gathering dispersed. The good burghers, the respectable suburbanites on holiday in the mountains, the local dairymen and landlords, returned to the weekend recreations they had foregone for a day because of their grave anxieties about their nation.

Similar meetings involving similar kinds of people had punctuated the summer throughout the United States. At all of them, as at Ascutney, the thousands who came and listened to speeches and asked questions at study groups, revealed their common concerns. Only a few years earlier, under the leadership of a president elected by an enormous majority, the federal government had initiated a stunning program of reform, appropriated unprecedented sums of money to attack poverty, to promote civil rights, to support higher education and access to it. Now the cities were aflame with the angry protests of the poor and the proscribed frustrated by the persistence of their lot; the campuses were at the verge of an explosion of impatience of the idealistic young; the unending war in Vietnam was absorbing national wealth and American lives for official purposes increasingly dubious and remote; the President could not move about the country without confronting hostile crowds.

The address and the workshops at Ascutney spoke to themes that marked the public discourse of the ensuing year, themes that moved millions of Americans—not just radical or rebellious Americans, but in far larger number, the comfortable middle class and many just plain folks—to force the president out of politics and to split his party beyond immediate repair. The war in

Vietnam, so went the argument at Ascutney, revealed an inversion of national priorities, a commitment to a singular and questionable end at the expense of multiple, more important goals. The earlier effort to reach those social goals had proved to be cosmetic and unsuccessful, as so often before in the national past. Radical critics, had they spoken, would have contended that reform within the system would never work, that state capitalism, American style, had to yield to a democratic socialism which alone could produce genuine reform. The speakers at Ascutney had not lost confidence in American liberalism, in gradual reform, but they did recognize its ambiguous results, if not always its ambiguous premises.

Those speakers and others elsewhere, then and through the following year and more, particularly attacked the distention of presidential power. They and their applauding audiences believed the presidency had become too strong. It had not always been so. About a century earlier, the comfortable, civic-minded middle class was beginning to recognize that the presidency had become too weak.

In 1880 James A. Garfield, an Ohio Republican congressman, and General Winfield Scott Hancock, a Pennsylvania Democrat and Union hero at the battle of Gettysburg, ran against each other for the office of president of the United States. Garfield had won nomination as a compromise candidate only after a sharp factional fight within his party. The resolution of that struggle provided him with a running mate, Chester A. Arthur of New York, who was notorious as a corrupt spoilsman. For his part, Garfield, a solid figure of Christian masculinity, had proved his personal bravery in war, his tactical skill in the House of Representatives, and his civilized intelligence. His campaign depended not on those qualities but on the tired sectional rhetoric of the bloody shirt and a lavish and unscrupulous use of money to buy votes. Hancock, who had held no elective office, displayed no less an array of personal credentials and no larger an investment in reasoned political debate or ingenuous election strategy.

Garfield won by a close popular vote but soon surrendered his conciliatory posture to the factional warfare waged by his influential secretary of state, James G. Blaine. Four months after his election the new President suffered a shot in his back from a disappointed office seeker. He died in September 1881, leaving the White House to Arthur who proved far better than his reputation but too ineffective to prevent Congress from extravagant expenditures or to persuade Congress to reduce taxes, including the tariff. After a Democratic sweep of the elections of 1882, the Republicans in 1884 rejected Arthur in favor of the fractious Blaine, a man of some talent and little integrity. Blaine lost another close election to his Democratic rival, Governor Grover Cleveland of New York, who was distinguished in the politics of his era for his persistent honesty.

In 1885, the year in which Cleveland took office, Woodrow Wilson published his doctoral dissertation, *Congressional Government*, a book that enjoyed a quick success. It provided an analysis of the presidency as well as of the Congress on which Wilson had been working during the Garfield-Arthur period and about which he had been thinking, directly or indirectly, for at least a decade. Learned about both English and American history, Wilson drew his conclusions from the remote as well as the immediate past, but the political developments of his own time much influenced him. He had been an observant boy when the House of Representatives impeached President Andrew Johnson in 1867, and the Senate almost convicted him. Wilson had been an undergraduate at Princeton when the scandals of the Grant administration were exposed, scandals implicating the President's associates and a number of congressmen, Blaine among them. Wilson was about to begin the practice of law in Atlanta, Georgia, when President Garfield allowed Blaine to resume the battle about spoils, and later, Wilson was advocating tariff reduction when Arthur's policies faltered on the Hill.

Congressional Government enjoyed the success it did partly because Wilson struck positions with which polite, literate, civic-minded Americans generally agreed. He was one of them, and they had shared his observations. The "prestige of the presidential office," Wilson wrote, "has declined with the character of the Presidents. And the character of the Presidents has declined as the perfection of selfish party tactics has advanced." The weight of factional politics distorted the process of nomination which then produced poor candidates who, upon election, could not overcome the dominion of the Congress. The presidency, Wilson continued, "has fallen from its first estate of dignity because its power has waned; and its power has waned because the power of Congress has become predominant." In support of his argument he cited the impeachment of Johnson. Doubtless he had also in mind the dominating role of Johnson's cabinet and, more recently, of Blaine: "Our latter-day Presidents live by proxy; they are the executive in theory, but the Secretaries are the executive in fact. . . . The President is now scarcely the executive . . . ; he appoints the executive." Neither Andrew Johnson or Chester Arthur had been able to prevent Congress from overriding their important vetoes, as Wilson knew. "The President," he wrote, "is no greater than his prerogative of veto makes him; he is powerful rather as a branch of the legislature than as the titular head of the Executive." As he put it elsewhere in the book, the chief executive was "simply charged with the superintendence of the employees," a responsibility, as his readers knew, discharged lately in the breach. Wilson saw no remedy. In 1885 he believed that the conditions he remarked grew out of the organic nature of public institutions. "The . . . inevitable tendency of every system of self-government," he then contended, ". . . is to exalt the representative body . . . to a position of absolute supremacy."

Congressional Government had begun to move through several editions by 1889 when President Benjamin Harrison appointed Theodore Roosevelt, an ambitious, young Republican patrician from New York, to his first federal office as a Civil Service commissioner. Less clinical and more passionate in mind and manner than Wilson, Roosevelt railed in private letters against what he considered the stupid obduracy of Congress and the partisan selfishness of cabinet officers most involved in distributing patronage. As he saw it, Harrison lacked the strength of conviction and intelligence necessary for a president. "Oh, Heaven," Roosevelt lamented, "if the President had a little backbone, and if the Senators did not have flannel legs!" He opposed Harrison's renomination; he found Grover Cleveland, who returned to the White House in 1893, little more satisfactory; and he had similar reservations, perhaps less grave, about William McKinley, under whom he also served. For Congress he felt an increasing disdain. "If this country," Roosevelt wrote in 1897, "could be ruled by a benevolent czar we would doubtless make a good many changes for the better."

At that time Roosevelt had an obsessive desire for expansion in the Caribbean and the Pacific, a course to which President McKinley soon came with the war against Spain and the ensuing territorial accessions. Both the war itself and the organization of empire brought about a discernible growth in presidential authority. In 1897 Roosevelt and other observers had also begun to understand the developing need for a larger growth in federal and in presidential power to cope with domestic issues of moment. As the century turned, special private interests, especially financial and industrial interests, held the dominant power over social and economic policies within the United States. Those interests had grown in strength and range for several decades. In that time the processes of industrial consolidation and of finance capitalism had resulted in enormous concentrations of private wealth and authority in transportation, mining, manufacturing and banking. The practices of the managers of those consolidations operated to the disadvantage of workers, farmers and small enterprisers. Further, the quest for corporate privilege and immunity ordinarily involved the distribution of valuable favors to corruptible public officials at all levels of government. The managers of wealth had at once helped to develop the American economy and provoked the anger and despair of the victims of that development. To quiet the resulting anxieties, to make private power accountable, and to restore the primacy of public interests required a deliberate restraint of the power of private interests, a task for which only the federal government had adequate scope and authority, as it had also for the redistribution of wealth necessary to correct the abuses which the developers had spawned. It was a sensitive task, calling for skilled advocacy and leadership, as well as for efficient execution—conditions that pointed to the potential primacy of the president as an agent of change.

Theodore Roosevelt and Woodrow Wilson came to perceive that possibility and its importance, and to foster the growth of the presidency, during the first two decades of the twentieth century, a period notable for the many efforts at political and social reform which that generation called "progressive." Roosevelt and Wilson made their marks on American government and on domestic and foreign policy as the first progressive presidents. Later, in the 1930's, under substantially different conditions, Franklin D. Roosevelt carried their beginnings much further. The three men reshaped the office of the presidency, used it intentionally to improve the conditions of life in America, and mobilized it in periods of major national involvements in world affairs. During the administrations of all three, the great questions of political reform related to the location and use of power in the United States, to the relationship between the power of private individuals and groups—businessmen and corporate entities in particular—and the growing power of the federal government; and within that government, to the changing balance of power among the legislative, the judicial, and the executive branch which was increasingly the strongest.

Theodore Roosevelt cultivated the development of federal and of presidential power. His large definition of his office influenced Wilson's perceptions of the presidency and established a foundation upon which both Wilson and Franklin Roosevelt built. The first Roosevelt also helped to turn government toward a course of moderate domestic reform designed to meliorate the unfortunate circumstances of social and economic life that had provoked strong agrarian and labor protests during the 1890s, and to contain the forces of industrial and financial combination that those protests had attacked. Committed to similar objectives, Wilson brought the program of progressive reform to its temporary peak. His efforts, like Roosevelt's before him, revealed the ambiguities unavoidable in any attempt to improve the American system of political economy without destroying it, unavoidable also in the nature of the American political process. Those ambiguities—ordinarily unacknowledged, often troublesome, but not necessarily crippling—persisted through the New Deal of Franklin Roosevelt. All three presidents confronted, too, other problems of power and of paradox in foreign policy. For the second Roosevelt especially, the need arose alike in depression and in war to decide how to order different and conflicting national priorities, all of which merited some, though not necessarily equal, attention.

By 1945 the progressive presidents had established a legacy for American liberals—a legacy of a strong chief executive, skilled in politics, engaged in promoting gradual social reform, and accomplished in managing international policy. Yet the legacy was less certain than it seemed. The progressive presidents themselves had on occasion misused their power, faltered in guiding social change, stumbled in international ventures. The ambiguities of liberalism remained, as did the mutual incompatibility, at least politically, of various causes at home and abroad. The rush of postwar change sometimes obscured the uncertainties of the legacy, just as clumsy presidential decisions continually exposed them. Harry Truman failed to convert his domestic program into legislation. John F. Kennedy died before he might have succeeded. But by 1964–65 Lyndon Johnson seemed to have put together again the ingredients of authority and purpose that had characterized the progressive presidents. And then by 1967 the uncertainties of the legacy had become naked as the ski slopes at Ascutney in August.

It was deceptively easy then to overlook the benefits in the tradition of the progressive presidents. The liabilities obtruded. Yet the contributions of Roosevelt, Wilson, Roosevelt—and Johnson, too—to American government and society had a continuing utility that potentially transcended a crisis born in part of a misinterpretation and misrepresentation of the legacy. Those gathering at Ascutney, in contrast to more radical or more defiant Americans, had come together not to scuttle a discredited system but to work within it, indeed to restore it to operable condition. That had been the purpose, too, of the progressive presidents.

THE
PROGRESSIVE
PRESIDENTS

I

Theodore Roosevelt and the Definition of Office

THE SPECIAL MARK OF THEODORE ROOSEVELT was joy—joy in everything he did. That quality animated his tenure as president. He craved the office, so much so that for many years he preferred not to let himself think about it lest his thoughts impair his judgment. During those years he overcame the prejudices of his privileged youth and mastered the volatile energies of his exuberant temperament. A New York patrician, educated as a boy in Europe and by private tutors, a somewhat foppish graduate of Harvard College, and yet an easy companion of the woodsmen and cowboys he befriended at his ranch in the Dakotas, Roosevelt learned gradually to work with small-time professional politicians whom he at first disdained. In order to win office and to make government function, he taught himself to restrain any politically dangerous impulse, to study complex matters of policy before dealing with them, and to balance his objectives against the likelihood of achieving them—an exercise he often obscured by clothing the art of the possible in the rhetoric of the imperative.

Roosevelt absorbed those lessons while he held a succession of instructive offices. In his first, as a member of the New York State Assembly from 1881–1884, he had to associate, as he put it, with "liquor sellers . . . a butcher . . . a pawnbroker . . . twenty low Irishmen," all Democrats. Satisfied that the Republicans had higher standards for public life, he made party regularity an instrument for his own advancement. From 1889–1895, as a United States Civil Service commissioner under Presidents Benjamin Harrison and Grover Cleveland, he observed the ways of machine politics while he strove to prevent their intended beneficiaries from receiving appointments to jobs he wanted to reserve for candidates of merit. His success in expanding the merit system persuaded him that the federal government was becoming capable, through recourse to a trained bureaucracy, of managing increasing responsibilities. As police commissioner of New York City from 1895 to 1897, he usually won the cooperation of men like those he had met in the Assembly for purposes similar to those he had pursued in Washington. As assistant secretary of the navy in 1897–98, he contained much of his own martial spirit toward Spain and of his acquisitiveness in the Caribbean and the Pacific in order to conform to the less strident temper of his chief and of President William McKinley. As colonel of the Rough Riders, he integrated into an efficient regiment the curious assortment of Ivy League athletes, cowboys, Indians, and western felons whom he had recruited. He accepted all of them as peers so long as they worked and fought as he did, in a good cause and without fear or fatigue.

As governor of New York, Roosevelt directed all he had

learned to leading the state toward modest social and economic reforms, each of which met the opposition of Senator Thomas C. Platt, the "easy boss" of the state's Republicans. Platt's sponsorship in 1898 had been essential to Roosevelt's election. More and more apprehensive about the governor's independence, Platt in 1900 removed him from New York by orchestrating his nomination for vice-president. Roosevelt had not wanted that empty office, but accepting the verdict, he campaigned vigorously that fall against the Democrats' popular William Jennings Bryan, while President McKinley looked on benignly from his home in Ohio. McKinley's chief strategist, Senator Marcus A. Hanna, fretted. "Don't you realize," he was said to have objected when Roosevelt's name moved into nomination, "that there's only one heartbeat between that damned cowboy and the White House?" So there was. But bored with his official duties, Roosevelt was looking ahead to 1904 when the assassination of McKinley in September 1901 gave him the prize ahead of his schedule.

Inheriting what he had long coveted, Roosevelt, then only forty-two years old, would not let the accident diminish his pleasure in the reward. "It is," he wrote his intimate, Senator Henry Cabot Lodge, "a dreadful thing to come into the Presidency this way; but it would be a far worse thing to be morbid about it. Here is the task, and I have got to do it to the best of my ability; and that is all there is about it." He had more than the necessary determination and ambition. He had, too, the experience of serving three relatively weak presidents in whose hands the federal government did not develop policies germane to the major issues facing the country. Ordinarily captives of their Congresses, those presidents and their counselors were also prisoners of conventional and outmoded ideas about the nature of the economy and the related role of the state.

While still governor of New York, Roosevelt had recognized the sweep of problems confronting the federal government. Expansionist that he was, he had welcomed the accession of empire in the Caribbean and the Pacific that followed American victory over Spain. The United States, he had long believed, deserved both the recognition and the responsibilities of a great world power. Though the acquisition of extracontinental territory signaled the emergence of the nation as a colonial presence, it did not in itself assure the status and the influence Roosevelt sought. It remained for the country to play a large role in world affairs, one he considered necessary both to assert American primacy in contiguous areas and to demonstrate American ability to prevent the domination of Europe or Asia by a potentially hostile power. For that role only the president had the necessary authority. With that view of international affairs Roosevelt had begun to define an equivalently large conception of the domestic responsibilities of the federal government, particularly those of the president. The states, as he had learned from experience, could not satisfactorily discipline the activities of large, national corporations. Existing federal legislation for that purpose, weak and vague at best, had failed of enforcement. The whole breadth of social and economic problems that the depression of the 1890's had exposed at their worst remained unresolved in the absence of a federal program of adequate scope, a program still to be fashioned, and of a federal executive equipped and empowered to give sinew to the law. Roosevelt yearned to grapple, as no president yet had, with the whole complex political and social agenda of modern industrial society.

When his chance came, Roosevelt, unlike his predecessors, had the will—the unappeasable will—to control any environment in which he found himself, the will to govern. He had brought his own person under a discipline so tight that he treated family tragedy—the decay and death of his brother—without pity, and suppressed private grief, after the death of his first wife, with mute fortitude. The public Roosevelt sought a comparable control over the processes of the federal government, marked as they were when he assumed office by continuing uncertainties about the range of authority of the three separate branches. Only the federal government, as he saw it, once organized to his prescription, could subdue the potentialities for turbulence in American life, those clashes of rich and poor, capital and labor, farm and city, that had agitated the nation during the 1890s. Within the government, only the president, in his view, could provide the direction to create and maintain a vibrant social equilibrium.

Roosevelt's delight in power, as well as his expansive conception of the presidency, imbued his intention to manage government and society. He gladly assumed responsibilities which his immediate predecessors had not thought to contemplate. "My view," he later wrote in a telling passage of his *Autobiography*, "was that every executive officer, and above all every executive officer in high position, was a steward of the people bound actively and affirmatively to do all he could for the people, and not to content himself with the negative merit of keeping his talents undamaged in a napkin. . . . Under this interpretation . . . I did and caused to be done many things not previously done by the President and the heads of the departments. I did not usurp power, but I did greatly broaden the use of executive power. . . . I acted for the common well-being of all our people whenever and in whatever manner was necessary, unless prevented by direct constitutional or legislative prohibition."

That assessment admitted less than Roosevelt knew about the constitutional and institutional restraints on executive authority that the Congress and the courts had created, particularly during the several decades before 1900. Yet as he realized, the unrivaled platform of his office—a "bully pulpit" in his phrase—imposed upon the incumbent an opportunity, one he deemed a duty, that no other officer of the government, no agency, no senator, no judge, could assume—an obligation to define the great national problems of his time, to propose a practicable solution for each of them, and to pursue those solutions with an educated sense of priorities. The president, Roosevelt maintained, could not do efficient work if Congress were permitted to make up his mind for him. Decisiveness was not enough, for the test of policy lay in implementation. "The bulk of government," Roosevelt observed, "is not legislation but administration." To that, as to the other demands of his office, he was continually alert.

Roosevelt was one of the most learned of modern residents of the White House. He had an historian's sense of the past, especially of the American past, about which he wrote zestfully and prolifically. He was an amateur authority on military and naval tactics and strategy. He was familiar with the great literature of half-a-dozen tongues. He was a creditable student of the biological sciences and an informed critic of scientific writing. He knew also how to solicit and accept advice. He invited to the White House poets and authors, inventors and explorers, economists, sociologists and ministers of the gospel. There came doers as well as theorists, lawyers, business executives, labor leaders, generals and journalists, all of whom Roosevelt probed for information and ideas. And there came books and journals on a multiplicity of subjects which he read with astonishing speed and retention.

His state papers, the products of his inquiries and ruminations, revealed a knowledge about domestic and foreign affairs which was unapproached, in the judgment of one of his associates, by any president before his time. Roosevelt was not profound or systematic. He was curious, educable and reflective. He made public statements that seemed spontaneous and sometimes impetuous, but there usually lay behind them hard hours or even weeks or years of study. In that sense he was an intellectual. That, in his opinion, was an indispensable adjunct to his being constantly a man of action.

Before coming to Washington, Roosevelt had concluded that the dominant issue before the federal government was its relationship with business. The proceedings of the Chicago Conference on Trusts of 1899 whetted his growing interest in that subject which he explored in a lively correspondence with experienced and expert men. Those he consulted stood, as he did, for gradual and moderate change designed to increase federal authority over corporate practices. Once president, he began to take to the people and the Congress his views about the consolidations of industrial wealth and power that his generation knew as the "trusts." For the academic authorities on the problems of competition, there was nothing new in his recommendations. He consciously borrowed his ideas from political economists like William Z. Ripley and Jeremiah W. Jenks who, with others, also influenced the findings of McKinley's industrial commission. Roosevelt consulted, too, with responsible and respectable business executives, some of them eager to enlist the government in the preservation of orderliness within industries private managers had been unable to stabilize. Compared to the demands of the radicals of the 1890's, of the Populists or the Knights of Labor, Roosevelt's proposals were as temperate as he labeled them. Still, what he said about government and business took into account the realities of the marketplace and of monopolistic competition. He spoke his mind continually and forcefully until both people and Congress were prepared to apply some of his favored remedies. In devising them, he broke with the doctrines of laissez faire economics, the doctrines in which he had been educated and in which most comfortable Americans believed, and he discomposed the stand-pat majority of his unadventurous party.

Roosevelt never dreamed of abolishing corporate capitalism. He dismissed socialism as evil and hateful. He also valued the contributions of corporations to national productivity and strength, and to what others would later describe as the modernization of the national economy. As he said, he had no quarrel with corporations that offended only because of their awesome size. Sheer individualism, in his formulation, could no longer serve as the basis for a society that had become rich and complex. In order to deal with corporate consolidations, ordinary individuals had to combine in associations of their own, like labor unions and farmers' cooperatives, and especially to rely on the largest of all combinations, the federal government. In its turn the government had to fashion the means to regulate the behavior of corporations, to prevent them from unfair pricing, from the marketing of shabby goods, from discriminatory competitive behavior, and from dominating activities that were properly the responsibility of the whole people and their political representatives.

Before the federal government could compose the rules or create the agencies to make corporations accountable to it, it had to demonstrate that it had the authority, the will, and the capacity to do so. That demonstration, as Roosevelt saw it, called for presidential leadership. It was up to the president to create investigatory and supervisory bodies within the executive branch or attached to it, and to staff them with officers competent for the task of writing and enforcing necessary social and economic legislation. It was up to the president to build a public consensus for his policies and to shepherd legislation on the Hill. The establishment of the authority of the federal government to act required the president to challenge prevailing judicial doctrines, perhaps even the courts themselves, and particularly the Supreme Court.

Roosevelt began by testing the Supreme Court's interpretation of the Sherman Antitrust Act of 1890, an act that declared illegal combinations and conspiracies in restraint of interstate or foreign commerce. "The absolutely vital question," he wrote in his *Autobiography*, "was whether the government had power to control" the trusts at all. The decision of the court in the E. C. Knight case (1895) seemed to say the government did not, for the court ruled that a monopoly in the refining of sugar did not fall under the Sherman Act because manufacturing, of which refining was one form, did not constitute interstate commerce. That decision,

Roosevelt asserted, "I caused to be annulled by the court that had rendered it." He did so by the successful prosecution of the Northern Securities Company, a corporation that held the controlling share of stocks in several western railroads. It was "impossible," Roosevelt believed, "to overestimate the importance" of that case.

The omissions, the inaccuracies, and the hyperbole of that statement—qualities rarely foreign to Roosevelt's retrospective assessments of his achievements—did not distort its essential truth. He neglected to say that before the decision he had tried to tilt the court in his favor. He construed the modification of an earlier ruling as a reversal of that ruling. He also overlooked two important aspects of his action: his selection for prosecution of a particularly unpopular target, a characteristic of most of his antitrust endeavors; and his general antagonism to all judge-made law that blocked his own policies.

The special issue of antitrust law constituted only one part of the general problem of judicial barriers to social reform. In the two decades before 1900 the Supreme Court declared unconstitutional a considerable body of state and federal legislation designed to rectify, in each instance modestly, the most palpable inequities in American life. The narrow interpretation of the commerce power in the E. C. Knight case limited the utility of the antitrust law, but the court approved of the use of that act to prevent labor unions from engaging in strikes against even intransigent management, a ruling that had negligible reference, if any, to the intentions of the Congress that passed the legislation.

Other decisions gave a constrictive definition to the due process clauses of the Fifth and Fourteenth Amendments. Those clauses forbade any deprivation of life, liberty or property without due process of law. Until the 1850's due process had been interpreted to mean due procedure, but during the 1880's and 1890's the Supreme Court fastened a substantive meaning to the phrase as it related to corporate property and laboring men and women. In that meaning the court held that neither legislation, no matter how fair and open the process of debate and deliberation, nor an administrative body created by law, no matter how fair and open its hearings, could make final decisions about prices or rates without taking into account sundry substantive issues, among them the questions of a fair return on and appropriate replacement value of capital. Each of those considerations was to be subjected to judicial review during which a court, ultimately the Supreme Court, could insist upon its own findings. That assertion of judicial supremacy at a time when courts were notoriously solicitous of business interests also applied to labor, for the Supreme Court ruled that, with rare exceptions, laws setting maximum hours or minimum wages or benefits deprived a worker of the liberty to contract to sell his labor on any terms.

The freedom of the poor to be exploited had an odd counterpart in the freedom of the wealthy from income taxes. Though the Supreme Court had upheld an income tax imposed during the Civil War, in a tortured ruling of 1895 it reversed that decision and held that a new income tax was a direct tax and therefore unconstitutional because it was not apportioned, as direct taxes had to be, among the states according to population. That decision blocked the rectification of gross inequities in the distribution of American income and wealth.

State courts displayed tendencies no more liberal than those of the supreme bench and federal courts in general. The impact of judge-made law on American life, and the successful assertion of judicial supremacy, frustrated the advocates of social progress. Indeed much of the progressive movement of the early twentieth century involved an effort, deliberate or incidental, to use non-judicial instruments of government to undo what the courts had done. So it was with Theodore Roosevelt, that most visible of progressives, whose objectives as president led him to appoint judges and prosecutors sympathetic to reform, to try through them to persuade the courts to overrule their burdensome decisions, and to sponsor federal statutes designed to restrict the range within which courts could thereafter rule.

Within that context, the Northern Securities case, as Roosevelt asserted, had an importance impossible to overestimate, for it was his first and unexpected assault, shocking to the lords of American finance whose power he impugned. The Northern Securities Company was formed in 1901, shortly after Roosevelt assumed office, to terminate a contest over control of the Northern Pacific Railroad which had pitted the interests of J. P. Morgan and James B. Hill against those of E. H. Harriman, the Kuhn-Loeb investment house, and indirectly the Rockefellers. Hill, an eminent railroader whose showpiece was the Great Northern, had purchased what he and Morgan, his ally, thought was a commanding share of the stock of the Northern Pacific. They wanted that road because it held a controlling interest in the Chicago, Burlington and Quincy, and its tracks provided an entrée into Chicago for the Great Northern. The three lines gave Hill a strong grip on transportation in the northwestern United States. His foremost rival, the comparably wealthy and ambitious E. H. Harriman, presided over the fortunes of the Union Pacific, a great line with routes through the central western states. Threatened by Hill's imperial merger, Harriman in 1901 retaliated by setting out to capture the CB&Q, a natural adjunct to his routes. To that end he began through Jacob Schiff quietly to buy up Northern Pacific stock. Alarmed belatedly by that raid, Hill and his agents from the house of Morgan entered the market to outbid Harriman and Schiff.

In the ensuing auction Northern Pacific reached unbelievable highs, especially after unwary brokers who had sold short were caught short and tried to cover. In their stampede for cash for Northern Pacific shares, they dumped other holdings at panic prices. The major contestants then decided that peace was preferable to the uncertainties of battle and the disorder in the market. They arranged an alliance by incorporating the Northern Securities Company to hold their accumulated shares in Northern Pacific as well as those of the other railroads involved in the contest. With the formation of the new holding company, the principals had in their grasp the entire transportation system of the northwestern quarter of the nation.

The episode provoked instant criticism. The irresponsibility of the former rivals in bringing on a stock market panic outraged even the *Wall Street Journal*. The creation of the huge holding company so soon after the chartering of the United States Steel Corporation, the first billion dollar combination, further alarmed the many Americans already frightened by the trusts. The new railroad giant struck shippers in the area, most of them farmers, as a monster that would swallow their profits in swollen rates. Those responses gave Roosevelt just the vulnerable target he needed for a first antitrust action. While the attorneys general of several western states either planned or initiated suits against the Northern Securities Company, the President preempted the opportunity by directing his attorney general to begin federal proceedings.

That prosecution, announced in 1902, ruffled the dovecotes of lower Manhattan. J. P. Morgan, incredulous, sent his lawyer, "his man" as Roosevelt put it, to see the attorney general, "my man," as if he could bargain with the President as an equal. Morgan was accustomed to operating that way. A private conference between his counsel and the Justice Department would have settled any troublesome matter in previous years, and there were sound financial and economic reasons to excuse the railroad combination. But Roosevelt did not propose to negotiate with any private citizen. Through the attorney general he assured Morgan that the federal government would not persecute him, but it would proceed against the Northern Securities Company.

Apart from its unpopularity, that company was in the business of interstate transportation. Though transportation was indisputably a form of commerce, some lawyers held that the Interstate

Commerce Act affected railroads and the Sherman Act did not. It was also unclear whether a holding company, incorporated under the laws of one state, New Jersey, constituted commerce, though obviously the operating companies it owned did. Those and other intricacies led the Supreme Court in its decision of 1903 to split by a vote of five to four. The majority, to Roosevelt's satisfaction, found the company in violation of the Sherman Act and ordered it dissolved. They denied that any device of organization, a holding company included, in itself provided protection against the intention of the act. They did not explicitly overrule the decision in the Knight case, but Roosevelt had won his point—the federal government did have some control over the trusts. The reach of that authority remained unclear, as did the court's definition of interstate commerce. Nevertheless the victorious President planned soon to attack again.

One unexpected development irritated him. Before the case reached the court, he had had the chance to appoint a new associate justice. On the advice of his friend Lodge, he selected Oliver Wendell Holmes, Jr., whose record on the Massachusetts bench had marked him as a man of special distinction of mind. Roosevelt looked upon Holmes as a fellow reformer who would support his ventures. He miscalculated. A profound skeptic, Holmes had grave doubts about the nature of man. The fallibility of judges, as of all men, he believed, made it incumbent upon them to deny the will of the people as expressed by their representatives as little as possible. But that doctrine of judicial restraint did not make Holmes a populist. On the contrary, he deeply distrusted popular passion. Accordingly he was wholly in character, though Roosevelt had misunderstood his character, when he dissented in the Northern Securities case partly because he believed popular passion was influencing his brethren. As he put it: "Great cases make bad law." For his part, Roosevelt told Lodge he was disappointed with Holmes.

The President did not on that account hesitate to use great

cases to prod the court to make what he considered better law. He undertook forty-four antitrust prosecutions, most of them against the largest corporations in the country, including the E. I. du Pont Company, the American Tobacco Company, and the Standard Oil Company. Each of those gargantuans dominated the industry in which it functioned. Each had earned the wrath of competitors, suppliers and customers whom it had absorbed or destroyed or bilked. Each, enormously profitable, sold products to millions of consumers who thought, often erroneously, that they were overcharged. For many years each had received unfavorable publicity, some of it unfair. Though each consisted of a rational combination of related business entities, and each benefited from superior management, all had long been unpopular and on occasion unscrupulous or overbearing. They had been accountable to no one. Roosevelt prosecuted those companies and others partly because they were vulnerable but primarily because he considered their behavior obstreperous.

The government won the important cases Roosevelt originated, though two of special significance were decided only in 1911 after he had left office. The court then found the tobacco and oil trusts in violation of the Sherman Act and ordered them broken up into several separate companies. Though the outcome little altered competitive conditions within the affected industries, the rulings in the American Tobacco and Standard Oil cases tried to establish a workable and comprehensible basis for the future application of antitrust law. Since there had existed no recognizable criteria for that purpose before Roosevelt moved against the Northern Securities Company, the court had marched a long distance down the path he had started to cut only ten years earlier, and on the way chopped down a considerable number of corporate bodies.

The decisions of 1911 left the court in command. Within the bounds of "reasonable contention," the justices held, the intent of the companies had been to create a monopoly. Their actions had placed an "undue restraint" on interstate commerce. Roosevelt, too, had focused on corporate actions or behavior. It was not corporate efficiency or the economics of scale and of verticalization to which he objected, nor did he oppose consolidations that prevented ruinous competition. What bothered him in 1911, as it would have ten years earlier, was the court's recourse to the words "reasonable" and "undue." They asserted the continuing supremacy of the judiciary in determining the question of reasonableness, and that assertion undermined the foundations of the system that Roosevelt, while president, had started to construct for the exercise of government's authority over industry.

In order even to propose the ingredients of such a system, Roosevelt had first to strengthen his own office. When he inherited the presidency in 1901, he recognized the weaknesses in his position. No incumbent since Abraham Lincoln had utilized the full powers of the chief executive; none since Andrew Jackson had done so in a time of peace. Roosevelt had to work with a Congress from which he could expect little cooperation from the Democratic minority and not much more from the Republican majority. The Republicans for some years had followed the adroit leadership of such staunch defenders of the status quo as Speaker Joe Cannon in the House and Senators Mark Hanna, Nelson Aldrich and John C. Spooner. Hanna also had a major influence on Republican party affairs which Roosevelt had to overcome if he was to gain nomination in 1904 and win a mandate of his own. The federal bureaucracy had grown in size and ability during the previous quarter century, but many of McKinley's political appointees in subcabinet positions—the scoundrels in the Post Office Department and the time-servers in the Interior for two examples—and in important regional offices lacked the probity or the energy or the intelligence Roosevelt considered essential to proper government. On that account, and also because of the lack of necessary enabling legislation, he could not acquire the information he needed about problems he deemed significant, including the disciplining of industrial behavior, nor could he count upon a crisp and effective execution of his orders. He could not properly either make or implement policy.

Roosevelt approached the removal of those obstacles with a wise sensitivity for his situation and with formidable political acumen. He mollified the oligarchs in the Senate by conceding them their preferences about the tariff and public finance, issues of major importance to them but of lesser interest to him. He also took over his party. Hanna, Roosevelt had commented in 1896, had "advertised McKinley as if he were a patent medicine." Now Roosevelt advertised himself. His pungent rhetoric, his joyful manner, his strenuous activity made him a hero to rank-and-file Republicans. So did his careful recognition of special interest groups—veterans, Catholics, Germans, Methodists, blacks, Hungarians, union leaders, Jews. His delicate distribution of patronage, now to a former opponent ready to be converted, now to a loyal friend eager to help, gradually wrested party control from Hanna. When Hanna continued in 1903 to decline an early declaration for Roosevelt's nomination the next year, the President forced his hand by making the issue public at a time when the senator needed assistance from the White House for his own re-election. Hanna, capitulating, openly withdrew his opposition to an endorsement of Roosevelt. The episode registered Roosevelt's success in becoming master of his own party, a condition, as he knew, indispensable for a president.

Meanwhile he had begun to appoint his own kind of men to senior federal posts and to press Congress for the legislation that would enable them to act. The latter at first required no substantial departure from the emerging consensus of congressional Republicans. In his message to Congress of December 1901, Roosevelt referred to the "grave evils" of big business and asked for "practical efforts" to remove them. He called specifically for legislation banning the granting of rebates on shipments of freight, for a bill expediting antitrust prosecutions, and for the creation of a new Department of Commerce which would include a Bureau of Corporations to collect and to publicize information about industrial conditions. The first two of those proposals stirred no significant opposition but they languished until the President undertook a speaking tour in the summer of 1902 during which he constantly attacked corporate privilege.

His program had less bite than his speeches. Railroad managers, as Roosevelt had learned by consulting them, wanted to cease granting rebates—reductions from published rates—which cut their profits. The rebates served the interests only of large shippers, like Standard Oil and the American Sugar Refining Company, which controlled so much traffic that they could extract favors from competing railway lines, as they systematically had. The Elkins Act of 1903, penalizing shippers who received rebates as well as railroads that.granted them, won easy majorities in both houses, as also that year did the Expedition Act which added to the antitrust staff in the Justice Department and speeded judicial consideration of antitrust cases.

The bill creating a Department of Commerce would probably have passed eventually in spite of conservative doubts about the proposed functions of the Bureau of Corporations. Early in 1903, however, Senator Matthew Quay, a Pennsylvania Republican who defended American business with the faith of a zealot, delayed the measure long enough to worry its sponsors. The President then resorted to his own evangelical techniques. John D. Rockefeller, he told the press, was bombarding Congress with telegrams denouncing the bill. In fact Rockefeller's lawyer had sent a couple of such dispatches, but Roosevelt's exaggeration roused public opinion and both houses of Congress then quickly fell in line.

The drama, both entertaining and effective, had less importance than did the fact-finding authority now seated in the new Bureau of Corporations and its companion Bureau of Labor. Along with other investigators, the staffs of those bureaus provided the information about business structure and operations, and about conditions of work that armed Roosevelt for the initiatives he took after he had won election in his own right. Earlier, in interceding to settle the strike in the anthracite coal fields in 1902, he had relied on the findings of the commissioner of labor in deciding to use his office on the side of the United Mine Workers, an extraordinary departure from the protection that presidents had long afforded to management. Similarly briefed, Roosevelt in 1905 approached the problem of railroad regulation. Since his was never a speculative or theoretical intelligence, his actions then revealed the conceptions about government and public policy that guided both his dealings with Congress and his efforts to facilitate federal control over business operations.

The President employed three tactics in behalf of the measure he wanted. He took his case against the railroads to the hustings where his speeches countered railway propaganda and, as usual, attracted large and enthusiastic crowds. Republican senators, especially those from the Middle West, increasingly alert to the growing sentiment for reform among their constituents, were reminded again of the enduring love affair between Roosevelt and most American voters. The President had already begun to mobilize support on the Hill by working out a kind of bargain, implicit to the principals, with the Old Guard in his party. He did so by appearing on several occasions to favor a reduction in the protective tariff. That was enough to upset men like Speaker Cannon for whom protection had the sanctity of religion. As Roosevelt expected, they were willing to follow his lead on railroad regulation in return for his quiescence on the tariff. Partly on that account, his railroad policy met no serious resistance from Republicans in the House of Representatives. In handling the Senate, the President played back and forth among progressives, moderates and Democrats until, after a long parliamentary minuet, he got exactly what he had recommended.

That legislation, the Hepburn Act of 1906, included many provisions of which one, vital in Roosevelt's judgment, empowered the Interstate Commerce Commission to prescribe, upon complaint of a shipper and after a full hearing, the maximum allowable railroad rate for the service in question. As the President knew, that was only a start toward his larger objective. He was reaching, still tentatively, toward a system in which continuous, informed and disinterested administrative action would supplant law suits and legislation, both discontinuous and inexpert, as the source for the regulation of transportation and industry. Even his request for endowing the ICC with authority only over maximum rates challenged the prevailing myths about the automatic beneficence of the free market and struck at the decision of the Supreme Court that had earlier denied the ICC that authority.

Roosevelt had asked for no more. His attorney general had advised him that legislation authorizing the commission to set definite rate schedules on its own initiative might be unconstitutional. "The one thing I do not want," Roosevelt wrote a critic, "is to have a law passed and then declared unconstitutional." Wisconsin Senator Robert LaFollette and other progressives also eager for more rapid and comprehensive reform, argued that Roosevelt was settling for a "halfway measure" that might discredit the principle at stake and damage the public interest. "I believe," the President replied, "in men who take the next step; not those who theorize about the two-hundredth step." He had said as much in his messages to Congress. He spoke "of the need of temperate and cautious action" in securing railroad legislation. The highway of commerce had to be "open to all on equal terms," he said, continuing: "It is far better that it should be managed by private individuals than by the government. But it can only be so managed on condition that justice is done the public." He concluded with his main point: "What we need is to develop an orderly system, and such a system can come only through the gradually increased exercise of the right of efficient government control."

The issue of maximum rates, the first increment in that graduation, occupied much of the Senate's attention during the debate on the Hepburn bill. It was bound to, for Nelson Aldrich, the elegant and influential Republican senator from Rhode Island, and others of the Old Guard, understanding Roosevelt's purpose as they did, opposed any movement toward efficient government control. They attempted to block the way by introducing an amendment to the bill stipulating broad judicial review of the substantive decisions of the ICC. For tactical reasons the President then briefly enlisted with another faction sponsoring an amendment specifying narrow judicial review, review only of the procedures of the ICC. Shifting parliamentary alignments brought him back to the moderate Republicans, less intransigent than Aldrich, who settled the issue by getting the bill through with no definition of the scope of review. That outcome conformed to the language and spirit of the President's messages.

Consequently Roosevelt believed he had won a great victory. So did many of his contemporaries. LaFollette and the minority of progressives who agreed with him believed Roosevelt had surrendered for half a loaf. Some of them, and some latter-day analysts, pointed to the patent inadequacies of the Hepburn Act. It did not equip the ICC fully to regulate the railroads, or to establish a specific yardstick for determining rates, or to forbid various methods by which privileged shippers could continue to extract the equivalents of rebates. The act did not diminish the economic power of the major roads. It was left for Congress during the next two decades to pass further legislation to effect those ends. But Roosevelt rejoiced because he had done what he had set out to do. Largely as a result of his own political virtuosity, he had obtained an act of Congress that reversed a crippling judicial ruling and that gave him the keystone on which he intended to construct his arch of federal control.

During the debate about the Hepburn Act, other reform legislation had begun to move through Congress. The most controversial of those bills authorized the Department of Agriculture to inspect meat packed for interstate or foreign shipment. In 1906 Upton Sinclair, an humane socialist and a master of the literature of exposure, published *The Jungle*, his racking novel about the filth and the vile conditions of work in the Chicago packing houses. Sinclair intended his book to ignite public support for better wages and protection for the workers. Instead most of his readers, revolted by his descriptions, developed a primary concern for safe meat. Federal inspection of the packing industry had long been a goal of Senator Albert J. Beveridge of Indiana, a confident imperialist, progressive Republican, and friend of Roosevelt. Now the President embraced that objective.

Roosevelt was no stranger to the issue. During the Spanish War he had enlisted with other officers in condemning the packers for selling putrid beef to the army. He had also recently received a report from the Department of Agriculture about meat packing, a report too bland for his satisfaction. In the spring of 1906 he commissioned another investigation, this time by two men he trusted, Charles P. Neill, the commissioner of labor, and James B. Reynolds, a socially conscious lawyer. The President encouraged Beveridge to proceed with the drafting of a meat inspection bill in cooperation with the secretary of agriculture. In May the senator introduced that measure as an amendment to the pending Agricultural Appropriations bill. It provided for federal inspection of meat packing, for the dating of all meat packed, and for charging the packers for the cost of inspection.

The major packers, the firms the public knew as "the beef trust," objected primarily to the latter two provisions. Their large markets in Europe depended upon a plausible certification of the quality of their products, which federal inspection would provide. They could adhere to reasonable federal standards more easily than could their smaller competitors, though those firms would be immune from federal oversight so long as they confined their business to intrastate commerce, as most of them did. But the major packers were worried about the possible severity of federal standards. Therefore they used their influence in Congress, particularly with the chairman of the House Committee on Agriculture, to try to prevent the dating of meat, to make the government pay for inspection, and to subject the decisions of the inspectors explicitly to judicial review.

Beveridge had the votes to prevail in the Senate but the House committee did what the packers wanted. Roosevelt then interceded. Urging moderation on Beveridge, he suggested that the Senate back off from the demand for dating. To end the stalling of the House committee, he released part of the "sickening" report Neill and Reynolds had prepared. It confirmed much of Sinclair's indictment and raised anxieties among the packers about their reputation in Europe. Roosevelt's threat to release the rest of the report moved the packers and their friends in the House to a compromise satisfactory to the President, though not to Beveridge. The House passed the bill with no provision for dating and none for charging the packers for inspection, but also with none for broad court review, the issue that most bothered Roosevelt. In settling again for half a loaf, he again took the half that affected the relationship between the executive and the judiciary.

The meat inspection and the railroad legislation had much in common. Both related to questions that had been under consideration for some years. Both passed in 1906 in part because data gathered by the federal government documented the need for remedy, in part because of growing public agitation to which Roosevelt contributed, in part because of his skillful leadership. Both increased the power of the federal government, though only gently, for in each case Roosevelt accepted the terms he deemed practicable instead of demanding stiffer terms he doubted he could obtain. Both acts also spoke to the scope of judicial review, which he considered fundamental.

At the end of 1906 Roosevelt had just started to build his system of control but he had lost his leverage with Congress. In the elections that year the Democrats gained enough seats to increase the President's difficulty in fashioning a majority for his program. That difficulty grew after the panic of 1907 frightened the financial community which characteristically blamed Roosevelt's policies rather than its own undisciplined speculation. So did the Old Guard on the Hill. Thereafter Roosevelt was able to move ahead, as in considerable degree he already had, primarily by appointing to public office able men who shared his goals, and by using his "bully pulpit" to broadcast his ideas.

Roosevelt's example, his style, and his administrative methods made it as easy as it was necessary for him to persuade dozens of impressively trained and dedicated men to enter the service of the federal government. In an earlier generation, such men had scorned public life, largely then the preserve of the party faithful who in the discharge of their duties too rarely exhibited purpose, intelligence or energy. Determined to invigorate government, Roosevelt gave public office a fresh mission, "to look ahead and plan out the right kind of civilization . . . to develop from . . . wonderful new conditions of vast industrial growth." His youth and vigor, his zest in experience and in people, captured the imagination of his contemporaries and of younger men who might otherwise have been content, as their fathers had been, with careers in law firms, banks and executive suites. Roosevelt's practice of delegating responsibility to those he trusted also attracted his recruits. Just as he believed in using the full powers of his office, so did he urge them to use theirs.

His cabinet included only a few weak men who presided over departments for which the President set policy himself. The others, as Roosevelt knew, could do their jobs themselves. Among them was Elihu Root, one of the most remarkable conservatives of his era, who directed the reform of the army he had begun under McKinley. He was succeeded by William Howard Taft, a judicious administrator and versatile diplomat. James R. Garfield as secretary of the interior brought learning and force to federal conservation policy. Attorney General William H. Moody, a skilled lawyer experienced in government, reorganized the Justice Department.

Below the cabinet level Gifford Pinchot, Roosevelt's Chief Forester and the most eminent of progressive conservationists, assisted the President in creating new national forests, withdrawing national timber and mineral lands from private exploitation, and preventing the categorical alienation of hydroelectric sites. Charles Prouty, Franklin K. Lane and Herbert Smith served as superior models of federal commissioners. The discerning critic of things American, Lord Bryce, had never in any country, he wrote, seen a more eager, more high-minded or more efficient set of public servants than those in American government during Roosevelt's administration. Naturally the President was proud of them. "Nothing could have been done in my administration," he recalled, "if it had not been for the zeal, intelligence, masterful ability, and downright hard labor of these men. I was helpless to do anything except as my thoughts and orders were translated into action by them; and, moreover, each of them, as he grew specially fitted for his job, used to suggest to me the right thought to have, and the right order to give, concerning that job."

That generalization applied to Roosevelt's persistent efforts to supervise the great industrial corporations. "We have the power," he said, "and we shall find the way." Much of the route lay through the Southern Judicial District of New York. Located in Manhattan, that district had unequalled responsibility for monitoring the large corporations, as so many of them had offices there. Nevertheless until 1905 the United States district attorney in charge had yet to prosecute successfully any case under either the Sherman Act or the Elkins Act. A McKinley appointee, he kept jumbled records, put in irregular hours of work, assembled a lazy staff, and in 1905 brought to trial only 27 of 610 active cases. The office, in the phrase of one commentator, was "in the last stages of bureaucratic paralysis." With help from Attorney General Moody, then recently appointed, Roosevelt in the fall of 1905 made the selection of a new district attorney a matter of cabinet business. He meant for lower Manhattan to feel his touch.

Among the outstanding Republican candidates considered for the post, the President leaned, as did Moody and Root, toward Henry L. Stimson, whom Roosevelt appointed after placating Senator T. C. Platt, still the state's "easy boss." Stimson, a member of Root's firm, was known to the President as a good horseman, an able lawyer, and a Republican of patrician origins and sensibilities like his own. After taking office, Stimson often received suggestions about prosecutions from the White House, but he always had the right to make his own decisions. From Moody he received a mandate to remake his staff. He brought in a group of young men of whom many, Felix Frankfurter most brilliantly, later became luminaries in public life. As Roosevelt did nationally, Stimson locally transformed the quality of public service.

Stimson and Moody also persuaded the President that the dispatch of business in the Southern District required the appointment of an additional federal judge there. While Congress proceeded with the authorizing legislation, they helped Roosevelt identify an appropriate candidate, Charles M. Hough, a lawyer of "a vigorous mind of high velocity" and "no illusions about corporations." In the three years after Hough took his seat, the prosecutions brought by Stimson and his staff changed the character of the district. As the foremost biographer of both Roosevelt and Stimson wrote: "A combination in restraint of trade was dissolved, fines of over half a million dollars were obtained from two corporations for infractions of the Elkins Act, eight officials of three corporations were fined or imprisoned for violations of the law, almost $3,000,000 were recovered from corporations that had by systematic fraud withheld these monies from the government. In the course of these prosecutions rulings were made on disputed points in the laws regulating corporations which, later sustained by higher courts, made the regulation of great companies easier in the future. Finally, the publicity obtained in these trials demonstrated to the citizens, as the President had wished from the beginning, the power of government to provide controls for the behavior of the new corporate energy."

Yet the adversary process remained too slow, and the courts too inflexible, for Roosevelt's taste. His disappointment with Holmes in 1903, his criticism of the rule of reason in 1911, revealed less of the intensity of his feeling than did an intermediate episode. Judicial nullification of a New York statute setting maximum hours of work in bakeries and of a federal employers' liability law, and judicial inhibitions on both strikes and boycotts brought the President by 1908 to a conclusion he would not have tolerated seven years earlier. "If the spirit which lies behind these . . . decisions," he wrote, "obtained in all the actions of the . . . courts, we should not only have a revolution, but it would be absolutely necessary to have a revolution because the condition of the worker would become intolerable."

Strong words, but Roosevelt expected reform to stave off revolution. He was coming to understand that an orderly industrial system required legislation assuring trades unions of the right to organize by protecting their right peaceably to strike or boycott, and legislation, too, setting reasonable standards for all labor of wages, hours and conditions of work. His annual message to Congress of 1908 contained the seeds of those recommendations which he made explicit in 1912 when he was again seeking the presidency. By that time he had also urged the recall through popular referenda of decisions by state courts, decisions of which many would, as he predicted, relate to labor cases. Though the prospect of recall, like the union movement, alarmed men like Root, Taft, and Stimson who had traveled part of the way with Roosevelt, those changes were wholly compatible with capitalism. Indeed, as Roosevelt argued, they provided the means to strengthen and preserve capitalism by making it more equitable.

Genuine revolution—an effort, whether peaceful or violent, to substitute socialism or syndicalism for capitalism—roused Roosevelt's unrestrained opposition. As president he condemned the objectives and the tactics of the syndicalist Industrial Workers of the World, he condoned repressive measures against their leaders, and he would have liked to close the mails to some of their circulars. He was equally hostile to socialists. Restless with legal precedents and procedures that protected the civil rights of dissident groups, he trusted his own judgment, volatile though it could be, more than he trusted the courts or even the Constitution. Mr. Justice Holmes, a wise spokesman for restraint, must often have been disappointed in Roosevelt.

The system of industrial control that the President described in his last messages to Congress—no previous president had had the experience or the insight even to venture such a description—required legislative and judicial recognition of the need for penetrating, though not arbitrary, executive power. Just as the Hepburn Act gave an administrative body partial authority over railroad rates, so Roosevelt proposed in 1908 and 1909 to empower a similar body with authority over industry. Administrative commissions, in Roosevelt's vision, would consist of thoroughly trained, politically neutral experts who would base their rulings on extensive, relevant data. Their continuous involvement in investigating industrial conditions would produce a wisdom and resilience that neither Congress nor the courts could provide. So long as they behaved properly, businesses, no matter how big, would have nothing to fear from the commissions, though they would have to learn to live with the much stronger union movement which Roosevelt encouraged as another counter to their power. Further to reduce the power of great wealth, he also recommended an estate tax to prevent the transmission of "swollen" fortunes and the favor they purchased, as well as a graduated income tax. In calling for social insurance in the Progressive party platform of 1912, Roosevelt completed his description of a proto-typical welfare state.

The expert, administrative commission, so central in Roose-velt's system, provided a less certain solution to the problem of regulation than he realized. Who were to become the experts, the philosopher kings? In his time less than a tenth of the Ameri-can people had access to the kind of education and professional training necessary for the role. Government by an elite of talent would be government by an elite of station. Who was to select the experts? Were the voters sufficiently wise and selfless to elect presidents who would appoint and senators who would confirm the paragons on whom Roosevelt's system depended? By 1912 he had come to advocate the democratization of political proce-dures—direct primaries, the initiative and referendum—but how were popular politics and elite government to be reconciled? What if the experts disagreed, or if they were wrong? What if they were not neutral but subject, like the rest of mankind, to the temptations of personal aggrandizement, or to corporate influ-ence, or to partisan pressure? Roosevelt urged the imposition of order upon industrial society so as to stimulate moral behavior, but the imposition and maintenance of order depended upon power, and though he had used his power on the whole respon-sibly, he had sometimes used it arbitrarily, just as his commis-sioners were likely to. His belief in power and his corollary impa-tience with any higher law presumed that governors, accountable to their constituencies only periodically, possessed astonishing wisdom, virtue and self-control. As much as anything else he did, his direction of foreign policy made that presumption dubi-ous.

"In domestic politics," Theodore Roosevelt contended, "Congress in the long run is apt to do what is right. It is in foreign politics, and in preparing the army and navy that we are apt to have most difficulty, because these are just the subjects as to which the average American citizen does not take the trouble to think carefully or deeply." As president, Roosevelt made it his mission, with little regard for Congress, to educate the average citizen. Much that he said needed saying, and much that he did merited respect, but his manner as well as his objectives often suggested that in managing foreign policy, he felt accountable to no one.

Roosevelt's countrymen harbored two illusions he intended to dispel: one, that the United States, insulated by the oceans and its own traditions, could avoid involvement in world affairs; the other, that peace was a normal international condition. Rapid changes in transportation, communication, and weaponry, so Roosevelt believed, had created a situation of potential turmoil in which only the availability of power and, when necessary, the application of force could assure a peaceful international order. The maintenance of that equilibrium, in his view, depended on the great powers and their dealings with each other.

Dedicated to American interests, Roosevelt had a soaring confidence in the benign nature of American destiny. One of the most ambitious expansionists of 1898, he also had a frightening infatuation with wars. From his field tent in Cuba he wrote with a perverse delight that "I got my Spaniard." Men of character, he constantly asserted, would prove their truth in battle. Indeed war purified character by testing it. It would eliminate the softness he found in modern life, the vulgarity of the new rich, the effete literature of expatriate intellectuals.

As president he employed a gentler rhetoric to press his case for preparedness. For him that state entailed the development of human and natural resources—hence his discourses about preserving mineral deposits, increasing the birth rate, cultivating physical fitness and the brave heart. Ultimately preparedness involved the armed services, their organization, size, equipment and command. Consequently he encouraged the reorganization of the army and undertook to modernize the navy, for which

Congress at his urging voted appropriations unprecedented in their magnitude.

Roosevelt's emphasis on the navy grew out of his enthusiasm for the doctrines of Admiral Alfred Thayer Mahan whose historical studies equated national greatness with sea power. American defense, Mahan and Roosevelt both believed, required a strong fleet with access to supporting bases from which it could control the Caribbean and the Pacific triangle with apexes at Panama, Hawaii and Alaska. National self-interest also generated an active concern for a balance of power to preserve stability in Western Europe and East Asia, and thereby to prevent the emergence in either area of a potential threat to the United States.

The foreign policies Roosevelt pursued to serve those ends distinguished between great power relationships with each other and great power responsibilities toward weak or unruly states. "More and more," he told Congress, "the increasing interdependence and complexity of international political and economic relations render it incumbent upon all civilized and orderly powers to insist on the proper policing of the world." He expected the United States to protect its hegemony in the Caribbean by policing the countries there. His motives were strategic but his actions took no account of the desires of the peoples they affected.

Roosevelt stated his rationale for interceding in the Caribbean in the form of a corollary to the Monroe Doctrine. Announced as part of his annual message of 1904, it had already operated as his excuse for intervening in Venezuela in 1902. Like many other Caribbean states, Venezuela had borrowed funds in Europe which its prodigal rulers lacked the means to repay. Great Britain, Italy, and Germany joined in a blockade to force the payment of debts due their nationals. Roosevelt objected to that exercise in an area he considered an American lake. Identifying Germany as the key offender, he warned the Kaiser to back off, and he ordered naval maneuvers to give credibility to his words. Germany drew back, the blockade ended, and for its part, Venezuela accepted the Europeans' demand for arbitration. Roosevelt then announced that in the future, preventive intervention by the United States in similar circumstances would make any European exercise unnecessary and unwarranted. "If a nation shows that it knows how to act with reasonable efficiency and decency in social and political matters," he told Congress in his message of 1904, a message intended for the world, "it need fear no interference from the United States. Chronic wrong-doing, or an impotence which results in a general loosening of the ties of civilized society, may in America, as elsewhere, ultimately require intervention by some civilized nation, and in the western hemisphere the adherence of the United States to the Monroe Doctrine may force the United States, however reluctantly, in flagrant cases of such wrong-doing or impotence, to the exercise of an international police power. . . . Every nation . . . which desires to maintain its . . . independence, must ultimately realize that the right of such independence cannot be separated from the responsibility of making good use of it."

On the basis of that theory, Roosevelt had sent American forces into Santo Domingo and later into Cuba. Those interventions restored order but fanned Latin American resentment of Yankee imperialism. The President's critics suspected that his corollary could easily serve as an excuse for adventures he initiated for other purposes. So it was in Panama. Long persuaded of the strategic importance of an isthmian canal, Roosevelt on the advice of an expert commission decided on a route through Panama. The engineers on the commission put forward convincing reasons for their preference for Panama over Nicaragua. The issue was nevertheless clouded because of the lobbying of representatives of the bankrupt French canal company who were zealous to have Congress buy their abandoned property. They did not influence the President, but he hurt his reputation by using one of them for his own purposes.

Roosevelt behaved imperiously on all counts. Panama was

then a province of Colombia which rejected the American offer for the purchase of a right of way. Roosevelt considered that response a hold up, though the Colombian legislature had every right and ample reason to seek a larger price. Rushing to go ahead, the President spurned further negotiations and instead encouraged a revolt for independence in Panama. On his orders American forces aided that revolt, and he at once recognized the new republic which quickly accepted American terms for the right of way. The Panamanians had long been dissatisfied with Colombian rule, which Roosevelt now conveniently described as disorderly. He had planned to seize the right of way if he had to, and to justify it as he then did.

"The experience of over half a century," the President told Congress in his dogmatic but implausible self-justification, "has shown Colombia to be utterly incapable of keeping order on the Isthmus. . . . The control, in the interest of the commerce and traffic of the whole civilized world, of the means of undistributed transit across the Isthmus of Panama has become of transcendent importance to the United States. . . . The government of Colombia, though wholly unable to maintain order on the Isthmus, has nevertheless declined to ratify a treaty . . . which opened the only chance to secure its own stability and to guarantee permanent peace on, and the construction of a canal across, the Isthmus." The United States therefore had no choice but to aid the Panamanian revolt. Accordingly, as Roosevelt later put it in his *Autobiography*, "I took Panama."

Roosevelt used a similar argument to condone the presence of the British in India and the Japanese in Korea. "To be sure," he wrote, "by treaty it was solemnly covenanted that Korea should remain independent. But Korea was helpless to enforce the treaty and . . . to . . . govern herself well. Japan could not afford to see Korea in the hands of a great foreign power. . . . Therefore . . . Japan . . . tore up the treaty and took Korea . . . and enforced order . . . carried out great engineering works . . . and doubled the commerce and the agricultural output." In the perception Roosevelt expressed, self-interest and stability took precedence over a treaty; efficient colonialism, over international law. The great powers would dominate their various spheres of influence.

Yet he also believed that the politics of power, as played by heads of major states, had to provide the wise restraints by which men lived. He found acceptable for American interests the balance of European power that existed at the turn of the century, but he became anxious about the growth of German ambitions. Had the Kaiser had the "instinct for the jugular," Roosevelt felt, he would have raised his guard against Russia. Instead Germany looked with equal or more suspicion and jealousy on France and Great Britain. Alert to the developing tensions and alliances in Europe, Roosevelt understood the severity of the crisis of 1905 over Morocco. The precise claims of the great powers involved there did not interest him, but he recognized the American stake in the preservation of a peaceful European status quo. Consequently he accepted an invitation from the Kaiser to urge England and France to negotiate. They agreed to, as they probably would have in any case. At the ensuing conference at Algeciras, the United States exercised little influence. The American presence was enough. It showed both the European and the American people that the president of the United States realized the importance for his country of any western European crisis. That message did not convince most Americans who remained indifferent to European affairs for at least another decade. Roosevelt, as he knew, would have shocked and angered them had he committed the country to any continuing participation in transatlantic politics.

Entirely on his own he moved close to such a commitment in east Asia. In the balance of power there he judged China, still weak and undeveloped, of no account, but to prevent contention among her neighbors he valued the fiction of her territorial integrity. Stability in the Orient, in his view, depended upon the offsetting strength of Russia and Japan. When the war between them broke out in 1904, Roosevelt worried about its "immense possibilities . . . for the future." A Russian victory, he believed, would be "a blow to civilization." Therefore he warned France and Germany that if they sided with Russia, he would side with Japan "to whatever length was necessary." Congress knew nothing of that pledge. By no means anti-Russian, Roosevelt thought that "her destruction, as an eastern Asiatic power, would also be unfortunate. It is best that she should be left face to face with Japan so that each may have a moderative action on the other."

Early Japanese success on land and sea, though expensive in men and money, forboded the imbalance Roosevelt feared. Consequently he agreed eagerly, at the request of both belligerents, to serve as peacemaker. The resulting Treaty of Portsmouth, which his negotiations shaped, cost Japan a large indemnity she had expected and cost Russia considerable territory she had wanted to retake, but the treaty ended the war. For his part in it Roosevelt won the Nobel Prize for peace. More important, the outcome fulfilled his purpose. "Each power," he concluded, "will be in a sense the guarantor of the other's good conduct."

The guarantee was uncertain. In spite of her backwardness and internal discontents, Russia had broad ambitions and enormous potential strength in Asia as well as in Europe. Accordingly Roosevelt applauded the Anglo-Japanese alliance formed to check the Russians. The President also had doubts about Japan. Emboldened by their victory, the Japanese might "enter into a general career of insolence and aggression." In the event the United States would not be able to defend the remote Philippine Islands, which Roosevelt had come to recognize as a strategic liability. Partly to obtain Japanese assurances about the Philippines, he conceded Japan's special interest in Korea in an executive agreement which he did not disclose to the Senate.

Roosevelt counted primarily on the navy to deflate Japan's ambitions. Yet sympathetic to Japanese sensitivities, he was dismayed when West Coast racism exploded in race riots that victimized immigrant Japanese laborers and spurred San Francisco in 1906 to pass an ordinance excluding Asians from public schools. Unable to control that city, the President had the State Department negotiate the "Gentlemen's Agreement" of 1907 with Japan. That understanding bound each country to stop unwanted immigration to the other. An agreement between equals, it also placated the Japanese. But Roosevelt used the crisis, with its accompanying loose talk about war, to convince Congress to accept his naval building program. He doubted that the Japanese really contemplated hostilities, but he also later claimed that he detected "a very, very slight undertone of veiled truculence" in their communications. That was provocation enough for him. "It was essential," he recalled, "that we should have it clearly understood by our own people especially, but also by other peoples, that the Pacific was as much our home waters as the Atlantic." To that end he ordered the fleet to sail westward around the world.

Roosevelt requested no congressional authorization to do so, nor did he have the funds for the voyage. He had enough to get the fleet across the Pacific, at which point, as he boasted, Congress would not deny him the money for the return journey. The Japanese welcomed the fleet to Tokyo Bay. Had they been bellicose, they could have blown it out of the water, or at least interpreted Roosevelt's tactic as a provocative act. In that event it would have been he, not they, whose truculence had endangered both peace and American ships low in fuel and thousands of miles from home. Fortunately instead the Japanese ambassador in Washington proposed a joint declaration of good will. Roosevelt nevertheless put his own, martial gloss on the episode. The show of force, he concluded, had had its intended effect. "The most important service that I rendered to peace," he wrote, "was the voyage of the battle fleet around the world." He was just as proud of his manner in ordering that voyage: "I decided on the move without consulting the Cabinet, precisely as I took Panama. . . . A council of war never fights, and in a crisis the duty of a leader is to lead."

In crisis and out, Roosevelt's strenuous leadership at home and abroad gave substance to his vision of his stewardship. He confronted the great issues of his time. "While President," he wrote an English friend in 1908, shortly before he was to leave the White House, "I have *been* President, emphatically; I have used every ounce of power there was in the office and I have not cared a rap for the criticisms of those who spoke of my 'usurpation of power'; for I knew that the talk was all nonsense. . . . I believe that the efficiency of this Government depends upon its possessing a strong central executive, and wherever I could establish a precedent for strength in the executive, I did for instance as regards . . . sending the fleet around the world, taking Panama . . . or . . . bringing the big corporations to book—why, in all these cases I have felt not merely that my action was right in itself, but that in showing the strength of . . . the executive, I was establishing a precedent of value. I believe in a strong executive; I believe in power. . . ."

Roosevelt therefore also believed that a president should serve no more than two consecutive terms. Since he would then be unable to renominate himself, the office would revert periodically to the people and remain responsible to them. That turnover provided less of a check on presidential power than he suggested. It did not require eight years or even four for a president to lead the nation beyond the edge of war, or to employ his "bully pulpit" to lie to the people, or to employ his authority to subvert the rights of individuals.

Roosevelt did none of those things. He might have if he had held office in more troubled times. He might have if Congress and the courts had relinquished their constitutional roles. As it was, in spite of his belief in power and his delight in its use, as president he practiced a self-restraint he often abandoned when he was seeking office rather than holding it. A model for strong presidents of the future, he succeeded, as they would have to, in winning the confidence of his constituency and control over his party, in bringing men of intelligence and probity into public life, in influencing Congress to enact much of his program, and in fashioning it according to a reasonable and persuasive ordering of national priorities. He recognized that the United States could not avoid involvement in world affairs and could not police the world alone. He understood that only the federal government could rectify many of the inequities in American social and economic life, and that the tolerance of American politics and culture ordinarily allowed only a gradual, though possibly a continuing, rectification. Those perceptions coincided with his sense of the special burdens of leadership and execution that fell to the president.

Roosevelt's definition of his office was neither final nor precise, any more than were his definitions of policy. Though he demonstrated the indispensability of presidential power, he left unresolved the issue of the proper limits of that power. He made apparent the significance of American military strength and of the nation's willingness to employ it, but he revealed the potential perils in his manner and extension of that use. He developed a system for the control of the industrial energy of the country, but that system contained no clear and democratic provisions for the selection and control of its managers. He made a thoughtful case for gradual and moderate social reform, but after leaving office he recognized himself that the gradualism then prevailing might not be fast or steady enough to keep up with social and institutional change. He never saw the paradoxes or the ambiguities in the progressive understanding of reform, ambiguities that would also face his successors.

Still Roosevelt left an impressive, if inconclusive, record. In his day his admirers and his detractors shared the national fascination with Roosevelt the man, Roosevelt the hero, Roosevelt the preacher, Roosevelt the president. While he was still in the White House, John Morley, an astute British observer, said it all very well. "Do you know," he asked, "the two most wonderful things I have seen in your country? Niagara Falls and the President of the United States . . . both great wonders of nature." So they were, powerful cataract and powerful man, sources of energy, creative in harness, rampant in flood.

2

Woodrow Wilson and the Ambiguities of Reform

MORE THAN SIX DECADES after Woodrow Wilson led the United States into the first World War—in his phrase the "most terrible and disastrous of all wars"—he remained identified with American liberalism, with the meliorative reform of progressivism and its extensions in foreign affairs. Whatever his failings, he phrased and symbolized some of the best hopes of that liberalism and its possibilities for the country and the world. In thought and behavior he also revealed many of the internal inconsistencies or ambiguities inherent in progressive striving. A strict moralist—Irish politicians who knew him called him the "Presbyterian priest"— he nurtured his political ambitions in uneasy harness with disreputable Democratic machines. A spokesman for commercial and political freedom, which his rhetoric continually linked, he subjected business to increased federal control and approved punitive barriers to radical dissent. An enemy of imperialism, he sent unwelcome troops to discipline weak nations. A prophet of peace, he went to war. Yet Wilson's confidence in the beneficence of his beliefs shielded him from the grave doubts about liberalism that war, revolution, and brutality implanted in other men, even in his lifetime.

Progressivism, never a neat or systematic creed, had almost as many guises as there were different groups of men and women, groups of divergent views or interests, who shared a general purpose, sometimes altruistic, sometimes selfish, to reform American society. Their several efforts sometimes clashed with each other, as did their several ambitions, especially in the frequent cases when high public office was at stake. Progressives in the House and Senate had broken with President William Howard Taft, Theodore Roosevelt's handpicked successor, whose policies on the tariff, conservation, and railroad regulation, among others, struck the disenchanted congressmen as too conservative. Roosevelt, who agreed, and in any case yearned to return to the White House, placed himself in front of the revolt of 1912. While the Old Guard in the GOP was managing the renomination of Taft, T.R. led his perfervid followers out of the convention and into a new party, the Progressive party, which nominated him on a platform dedicated to political and social reform. The real contest that year lay between Roosevelt and Wilson, a life-long Democrat who had needed the support of reformers within his party for his nomination and sought liberal support more broadly in his national canvass for election.

During their campaign Roosevelt and Wilson expounded their disagreements, though their areas of agreement were just as significant. Both candidates rejected the Republican platform which stood for preserving the status quo. Both opposed all radicals, including the Socialists. Both urged reform within the American political and economic system; both supported the democratization of political processes and the strengthening of trades unions. They disagreed about Roosevelt's proposed system for federal control of industry and about the prototypical welfare state his platform described. Concerned while president more with structural than with social reform, Roosevelt by 1912 had come to support redistributive taxation and federal social insurance. Wilson, skeptical about federal authority, still retained his southern and Democratic concern for states' rights. He also constantly attacked "regulated monopoly," his name for Roosevelt's proposed system, and advocated instead "regulated competition," his plan for precise legislative definition and vigorous legal prosecution of unfair business practices. He intended thereby to keep the economy open to competition, especially to protect opportunity for new enterprises, for men "on the make," whose prospects, he believed, would benefit also from a reduction in the tariff.

With the Republican party split, Wilson won an easy victory in the electoral college but only a plurality of the popular vote. The Democrats also elected majorities in both houses of Congress. That outcome gave the party a mandate to govern, the first it had enjoyed in twenty years, just as the combined vote for Wilson and Roosevelt provided reform with a mandate of its own. The new President, drawing upon only a few years of experience in public life, had now to decide how to use his office and his influence, questions to which he had, as a scholar and teacher, given much thought.

In his youth Wilson had liked to imagine himself a United States senator. That office would have allowed him scope for the oratory he enjoyed, and won him the recognition, perhaps the fame, he craved. After graduating from Princeton, he studied law, as did so many aspirant senators, and practiced briefly in Atlanta. The principles of law attracted him, but the pettiness of practice did not. Changing course, he entered the graduate school at the Johns Hopkins University where he earned his doctorate in political science. His dissertation, published in 1885 as *Congressional Government*, won considerable acclaim, as did several of his later books which he wrote while a professor successively at Bryn Mawr, Wesleyan of Connecticut, and Princeton. His publications revealed his admiration for great national statesmen, Washington and Lincoln in particular; his transcendent faith in America; his belief in the orderly, organic growth of political institutions; his satisfaction with conventional laissez faire economics—but also his worries about the power of great corporations and the difficulties of regulating them; his concern about the ineptitude of Congress and his disdain for the ordinary congressman; his contrasting affection for the British system of cabinet government; his distrust of recent immigrant groups; his horror of radicalism; and his longing for a persuasive national leader whose wisdom and eloquence "by methods which would . . . alienate individuals" would "master multitudes" and teach them to "keep faith with the past" and therefore to embrace "the progress that conserves." He intended to be that leader.

Those convictions undergirded his educational program while he was president of Princeton. His reforms there drew national attention, as did his eloquence in presenting his views. Frustrated by the university politics that eventually blocked his plans, he accepted the invitation of an influential group of anti-Bryan Democrats to sponsor his nomination in 1910 for governor of New Jersey. During his campaign for that office, he had a first direct exposure to the issues then agitating the electorate, issues central to the growing progressivism of the state. Sensitive to the mood of the voters and responsive to the advice of reform Democrats, Wilson began to move into the progressive camp, a movement that continued throughout his term as governor and his concurrent campaign for the Democratic presidential nomination in 1912.

As governor he built a progressive record by operating through a coalition of reformers from both major parties. The laws they passed provided, among other things, for the direct primary, for a commission to set intrastate railway rates, and for stricter rules for the incorporation of holding companies. That record and Wilson's methods for achieving it alienated the leaders of the Democratic regulars in New Jersey, but his national campaign managers constructed a coalition of their own that included both self-interested party men and progressive Democrats. With the nomination in hand and his party united in its quest for victory, Wilson then gave a progressive cast to his successful contest with Roosevelt.

Once president, Wilson decided to govern through his party, to rely not on a coalition of reformers but on the Democrats to put his program through, and in the process to broaden his party's base and strengthen it for the future. That decision rested upon his own theories of government and his accurate reading of political possibilities. Wilson believed that the party discipline upon which a British prime minister depended in Parliament could be imposed on Congress by a strong president. He knew that senior Democrats, most of them southerners, who chaired important committees in both houses had a telling influence on legislation but also reservations about his policies. To keep those Democrats in line, he appointed to his cabinet Postmaster General Albert S. Burleson, a former Texas congressman, and others experienced in the use of patronage, for which the Democrats were hungry. He planned also to be the persuasive leader of his own previous definition. But his decision to work through his party carried serious risks for reform. Just as Theodore Roosevelt had had to surrender some part of his purpose to the need for Republican support, so would Wilson have to accommodate to the tolerances of congressional Democrats still wedded to an orthodoxy about national policy that he had abandoned. The national parties had consisted for many years of informal coalitions of interest groups.

For even longer congressmen had had to be sensitive to the interests of their own constituents as well as to those of the nation. In the circumstances, the Democrats in Congress might be brought to support Wilson's proposals, but not without concessions which were bound to alter them. As had Roosevelt eight years earlier, Wilson would have to adjust to congressional politics. He could not expect partisan or congressional politics wholly to adapt to reform.

Yet he really had no choice. Roosevelt's unsuccessful effort in 1912 to surmount party politics by destroying his party had once again demonstrated the difficulty, if not the futility, of escaping the constrictions of the major parties as they had developed for almost a century. Further, the machinery of Congress, like the nature of American politics, did not lend itself to government by coalition. Only Democrats controlled the crucial committees. They were, to be sure, unaccustomed to governing after almost two decades in the opposition, but for practical purposes, their power in Congress was more important for Wilson's success than were their predictable but probably manageable disagreements with him. The President, moreover, had no substantial basis for forming a coalition. The regular Republicans opposed his policies. The handful of Progressives had a first interest in trying to build up their infant party and a fervid loyalty to Roosevelt. The Republican reformers who had stayed in their party and also held their seats were too few in number and weak in influence for Wilson to court at the risk of offending those doubtful Democrats whose votes he needed.

Committed on those counts to party government in spite of its liabilities, Wilson displayed impressive virtuosity in its execution. Respecting Congress as he did, he devoted himself to persuading his fellow Democrats, in private conferences as well as in official speeches, of the merit of his objectives. The absence of any dominating figure among Democrats on the Hill doubtless eased his task. His disposition of favor and his restrained view of reform held the southern Bourbons close to his purpose. He employed similar tactics to keep the representatives of the Democratic city machines in line. Southern and western agrarians, often disposed to move beyond his goals, usually yielded, though restlessly, to the counsel of compromise of their friends in Wilson's cabinet, in particular Secretary of State William Jennings Bryan. But Wilson's attitude and manner also served him well. "Congress," he wrote a friend early in his administration, "is made up of thinking men who want the party to succeed as much as I do, and who wish to serve the country effectively and intelligently. They have found out that I am honest . . . and accept my guidance because they see that I am attempting only to mediate their own thoughts and purposes . . . I am not driving them." Lead or drive, as the progressive *New Republic* judged in 1914, Wilson restored the prestige of the presidency which had slumped under Taft: "He has not only expressly acknowledged and acted on this obligation of leadership, as did Mr. Roosevelt, but he has sought to embody it in constitutional form."

He had begun with his inaugural address in March 1913 which summoned "all honest men, all patriotic, all forward-looking men" to his side. It also called for the reduction of the tariff, reform of the banking and currency system, and restrictions on the trusts. The two former issues he referred sequentially to the special session of Congress he convened. As had no president since Jefferson, Wilson addressed that Congress in person. He did so, he said, to demonstrate that the president was "not a mere department of the Government hailing Congress from some isolated island of jealous power." He then urged the elimination of tariff protection behind which the crudest American industrial combinations could organize monopoly. "The object of the tariff," he said, "must be effective competition." He proposed to eliminate artificial advantages in order to put to business the necessity of efficiency and to open opportunities for new ventures.

Tariff reduction, a traditional Democratic promise, had particular saliency in 1913. The tariff enacted in 1909 during the Taft administration had increased already high protective duties. The fierce debate over that tariff bill, a debate that pitted Democrats and progressives against the Republican Old Guard, had begun the disintegration of the Republican party and had echoed through the following years. In that time the Democrats made capital of the rising cost of living which they attributed to the Republican tariff. Democrats in Congress also formulated a series of bills, each of which reduced the duty on a controversial schedule. Though never enacted, those bills, taken together, provided the basis for the general tariff legislation that southern Democratic committee chairmen worked out in consultation with Wilson after his election. The resulting measure reduced average *ad valorem* rates, added various consumer goods to the free list, and removed protection from iron, steel, and other products of the "trusts." To compensate for the loss in revenue, the bill levied a modest graduated income tax,—the top rate was only three percent—which the recent ratification of the Sixteenth Amendment had made constitutional.

Involved in framing the bill, Wilson proceeded to guide it through Congress. No obstacles arose in the House, but in the Senate Democrats from states that produced sugar and wool endeavored to remove those commodities from the free list. With a majority of only three, the party could not afford to lose the votes of those senators or to invite logrolling on their part. Wilson therefore demanded the allegiance of the wavering men as a matter of party policy. In a speech to the nation, he also urged public opinion to "check and destroy" the "intolerable burden" of "insidious" lobbyists working for special interests. That appeal provoked the Progressives in the Senate to propose the divulgence by all senators of personal holdings affected by the bill. In its turn the disclosure persuaded one of the three embarrassed senators to support the bill which was enacted after progressives in all parties forced a compromise that doubled the surtax on personal incomes, though even the revised rates remained nominal.

With enviable flair, Wilson had used his office and his party to effect the only substantial tariff reduction of the century. Though the tariff, contrary to the implications of his arguments, was not "the mother of trusts," enough Americans thought it was and thought, too, that its rates correlated with the cost of living to assure applause for the President as a reformer. In some degree he was, but he showed little interest in the income tax included in the legislation. He did not engage himself in the successful effort to increase it; he did not much ponder about the social possibilities of deliberately redistributive taxation; he did not in later years participate in the framing or advocacy of that kind of taxation which Democratic congressional leaders made a part of national defense and wartime policy. In those respects he was not unlike the many progressives whose incomes fell within the top quarter of the national range. Many of them had a live interest in social justice; relatively few of them were prepared to pay for it. The President in 1913 made tariff reduction, an important but traditional objective, not social reform, his target, and he won. "I have," he wrote, "had the accomplishment of something like this at heart ever since I was a boy."

He had already put to Congress the problem of restructuring the nation's outmoded and inadequate banking system. The United States alone of all industrial nations had no central bank, no established machinery to manage currency and credit in order to help the economy respond to changing commercial conditions. That lack had intensified the panic of 1907 and then brought Congress to appoint a commission under Nelson Aldrich to make recommendations for remedy. Several years later Democrats in the House undertook an investigation of American finance that provided documentation for their suspicion that "Wall Street," a small group of eastern investment bankers, constituted a "money trust" which controlled industrial investment and much of the nation's industry itself. That conclusion, like the events of the panic of 1907, seemed to confirm the charges William Jennings Bryan had broadcast in his celebrated campaign in 1896, charges against the eastern bankers, their precious gold standard, and their manipulations of money and credit to the disadvantage of the folk. But both Bryan, now Wilson's secretary of state, and his large following of Democrats in Congress, had little enthusiasm for the recommendations of the Aldrich commission.

Wilson realized that there would be no banking legislation unless he could adjust the proposals of the commission to the demands of the Commoner. Aldrich sought to create a new institution that would rationalize American banking; Bryan, to use the federal government to reform the conditions of credit that favored the wealthy and penalized the small businessman and rural folk. Initially Wilson stood with the rationalizers. They had advocated the establishment of a privately controlled central bank, like the Bank of England, which would determine interest rates and issue currency on its own liability, as well as serve as the depository for federal funds. Even conservative Democrats favored federalizing that plan by creating a central supervisory board with enough regional banks to serve all parts of the country, including the predominately agricultural West and South. Wilson approved of that modification. His progressive counselors, Bryan among them, insisted upon further, more fundamental changes. The President accepted two: one, opposed by high finance, made appointments to the central supervisory board, the Federal Reserve Board, the right of the government rather than the bankers; the other, dear to Bryan, made bank notes the obligation of the United States, not of the central banking system.

Southern agrarians in the House demanded further significant amendments including explicit provision for the discounting of agricultural paper, the prohibition of interlocking directorates—presumably the tool of the "money trust"—and, most important, public rather than banker control of the regional reserve banks. Operating through Bryan, Wilson conceded enough to win the necessary votes. He endorsed the first point, promised later to attend to the second, and ignored the third. So amended, the measure alarmed Senate conservatives who prolonged hearings on the bill in order to open a forum for the hostile American Bankers Association. That pressure, as well as their own biases, swayed several Senate Democrats whose support Wilson had to have. He reminded one of them of the necessity for party discipline. He appointed a relative of another to a juicy federal office. He reached them all by claiming in a public statement that Wall Street was spreading artificial fears of a panic in an effort to defeat the banking bill. He also made no attempt to resist conservative amendments that reduced the power of the Federal Reserve Board and increased the proportion of gold reserves required for the issuance of bank notes. In that form Congress passed the Federal Reserve Act which Wilson signed in December 1913, only nine months after taking office.

The most significant domestic legislation of Wilson's administration, the new law evoked almost universal praise, as did the President for his role, "a great exhibition of leadership" in the judgment of a leading Republican newspaper. The Federal Reserve Act achieved much that he had wanted, the establishment of an efficient banking system, provision for greater flexibility of currency and credit, and creation of larger opportunity for equitable business loans to farmers and hopeful enterprisers.

Yet the artfulness of Wilson's performance in helping to devise the measure and in seeing it through Congress exceeded his claims for the results. Contrary to his description of purpose in his address to Congress proposing the act, it did not prevent concentration "in a few hands of the monetary resources of the country," nor did it place "control of the system of banking . . . in the government itself." The Federal Reserve Board had some control, but the regional banks, especially the Federal Reserve Bank of New York, the richest bank, exercised as much and sometimes more, especially over interest rates. According to the act, moreover, the officers of the regional banks were to be elected by the member banks of each region. In New York that provision sustained the influence of the great houses Bryan knew as "Wall Street." Further, though the President had the authority, with the consent of the Senate, to appoint the members of the Federal Reserve Board, the candidates he could locate were, with few exceptions, themselves bankers or men sympathetic to the views of bankers. Had he found and nominated less conventional candidates, the conservative Democrats on the Senate Banking and Currency Committee would have had the power to reject them.

The banking act represented a triumph for that aspect of progressivism that sought to rationalize American institutions, to impose order—as Theodore Roosevelt had tried to—on sporadic turbulence, in this instance on national finance. Though the act also eased the conditions of credit for small business, it did not decrease the advantages enjoyed by larger concerns, many of which financed their own growth out of their profits. The reform provided by the act was structural in nature, not social. Wilson was not alone in his ambiguous interpretation of those different effects, for the vocabulary of progressivism gave either or often both meanings to the word "reform." So, too, like most reformers, Wilson considered the control exercised by a federal board or agency a safeguard for the public interest, "control . . . in the government itself." But the public interest depended on the appointment to those boards of learned, disinterested, and judicious members, of whom there were never enough who were also acceptable politically, as Wilson's experience was to demonstrate.

The President moved further toward a reliance on federal commissions during 1914. He referred to the Congress the issue of government regulation of business and industry, the remaining item on the agenda of the New Freedom. He had found his party, like Americans in general, divided about the matter, and his address opening the new session of Congress revealed his own uncertainties. Interpreting "the best business judgment" to condemn monopoly, Wilson also acknowledged the unavoidability of large size in industry and the consequent utility of the holding company as a device of business organization. He proposed to prohibit neither, but to prevent monopoly or its equivalent by proscribing interrelated banking or management groups from controlling the major firms within an industry. Congress, he said, should specifically forbid that and other unfair business practices. The resulting definition of the meaning of the Sherman Act would then guide business activity and encourage healthy competition. Wilson noted, too, the need for administrative as well as legislative participation in the process of regulation. He proposed the creation of a commission to assist in the dissolving of corporations found to be in restraint of trade and perhaps to advise businessmen about the intent of the antitrust laws.

The Democratic leadership in the House made the party's measure the Clayton bill which expressly forbade interlocking directorates and other unfair practices. A separate bill set up an administrative commission with little more than the authority previously invested in the Bureau of Corporations it was to replace. For a time, the House program appeared to satisfy the President. He changed his position while the Senate was delaying action on the issues. Influenced largely by Louis D. Brandeis, Wilson in June 1914 gave his support to a measure Brandeis had drafted to establish a Federal Trade Commission authorized to prevent the unlawful suppression of competition. Brandeis, a brilliant lawyer and reformer and an advisor to Wilson in 1912, had tempered his own earlier advocacy of dissolution as an essential preventative of corporate misbehavior. His proposal of a strong regulatory commission brought him and Wilson closer than they had been two years earlier to the position of Roosevelt. Leaving the Clayton bill to its fate, the President employed his influence in behalf of the creation of the FTC.

Congress enacted both measures, but with portentous amendments. The prohibition against corporate mergers in the Clayton Act was modified by a coalition of conservatives to apply only in cases where those mergers tended to decrease competition, a vague standard subject to judicial review and definition. So, too, with Wilson's approval, conservative Democrats in the House made the exemption from the antitrust laws which the Clayton Act granted to labor unions, as the party's platform had promised, applicable only when the unions were engaged in lawful activities, again a standard open to the courts' interpretations. Wilson, furthermore, raised no objection to a Senate amendment to the FTC act that stipulated broad judicial review of the commission's cease and desist orders. As a consequence of those amendments, the courts could and did vitiate the legislation. During the ensuing two decades, while the concentration of American industry proceeded ever more swiftly on its former rounds, the Supreme Court exhibited no new vigor or acuity in its applications of the antitrust laws to corporations. In the name of those laws, lower federal courts, encouraged by the rulings of the supreme bench, issued more injunctions against labor unions than they had during all of previous American history. The Supreme Court also reviewed the orders of the FTC so as effectively to deny that commission any useful regulatory function.

Yet with the enactment of the antitrust laws Wilson considered his initial mission accomplished. Those laws, along with the tariff and banking acts fulfilled, he said, his "single purpose . . . to destroy private control and set business free." He never appeared discontented with the customary, broad power left to the courts. His own legal training made him respectful of both judges and the law. His program of 1912 envisaged a definition of the law intended to guide but not to inhibit the courts. Unlike Roosevelt, he had not set out to aggrandize the presidency at the expense of the Congress or the bench.

For its part, Congress responded to Wilson's leadership and party discipline without surrendering its authority. Independently of the White House, Democratic reformers and conservatives alike left their different stamps on the legislation of 1913–14. The conservatives went on to block the only clearly progressive nomination to the FTC that Wilson tried to make, George Rublee, who served only for the duration of a recess appointment. Apart from judicial review, the disposition of the Senate and its voice in appointments determined the spirit with which administrative agencies could exercise their mandates. The creation of the FTC restructured the terms of the relationship between government and business, but the members of that commission for many years made no rulings of much significance for business organization or behavior.

A disparity between form and substance also characterized Wilson's proposal of 1916 for a tariff commission. The Progressives had contended that such a commission of experts would bring science to tariff policy. Wilson and the Congress were more concerned about the prevention of a postwar flood of cheap European goods into the American market. As it worked out, the commission that was authorized and appointed ordinarily reported in favor of higher duties, a boon to American business. To be sure, the work of the commission increased the range of federal authority and satisfied the progressive faith in expert or scientific government, but the activities of the commission challenged whatever economic reform inhered in the tariff of 1913, so manifestly Wilson's tariff. Even he seemed ambiguous about what constituted a progressive course.

Other ambiguities marked the President's tenets. His appeal in 1912 for energetic enforcement of the antitrust laws attracted those progressives who felt, as he did, that the large institutions of industrialism imposed malign constraints on freedoms common to Americans in an earlier, golden, pastoral time. Even Roosevelt shared the nostalgia for country life and rural virtues. Yet just as Roosevelt had seen no way to abolish industrialism and the wealth and convenience it produced, neither did Wilson. Both men felt the contrast between rural and industrial values. Along with most progressives, most reformers, they wanted to resolve that conflict by infusing contemporary industrial society with the ancient truths, a paradoxical task. They proceeded by focusing on behavior. So Roosevelt condemned not industry but the "male-factors of great wealth" and Wilson proposed to punish not corporations but their managers, as he put it in 1912, to "make guilt personal." So Roosevelt called for the "vigorous life," the continuous engagement of moral men and women in their callings, and Wilson, employing a different vocabulary, admonished himself to "push on, to linger would be fatal." Like Roosevelt, he expected virtuous men to behave the same way, and when qualified, to do so in public life.

From that presumption and others related to it, there flowed still another ambiguity. Wilson believed, as did most other progressives, that men of talent and character should govern. Like many other progressives, he doubted that much talent or character existed outside of the ranks of old stock Americans, or even among the unsuccessful of that group. So it was that he looked to the elite in order to recruit an elite to public life; he wanted, as he said, to "put Princeton in the nation's service." Further, like Roosevelt and most progressives, he believed the majority should elect their governors even though he had apprehensions about the wisdom of the majority. He resolved that paradox by postulating, as Roosevelt had, that the American majority, whatever its failings, would elect men like him, men who could move multitudes but also govern well, "good men" who would appoint to office other good men.

Of all federal offices none more required the qualities of probity and intelligence, of a trained and agile mind, than did the justices of the Supreme Court. When a vacancy on the court opened in 1914, Wilson filled it with his attorney general, James C. McReynolds. He could scarcely have made a more unfortunate choice. McReynolds had friends in the Senate but few, if any, in the cabinet whose members found him testy, even mean. He had some reputation as an enemy of the trusts, but the President should have seen through that reputation. As attorney general, McReynolds invited large corporations to solicit the friendly counsel of the Justice Department in assessing the legality of their intentions. Several of them did so and came away on terms that suited them and avoided prosecutions. Those settlements, perhaps tougher than outright indulgences, revealed McReynolds as less than zealous about busting trusts. With little zeal either for the New Freedom, he urged Wilson in 1914 to assume a gentler stance toward business. Had the President inquired, he would have found that McReynolds, a fundamentalist in religion, read the Constitution as literally as he read the Bible. Wilson did not search that deeply. Perhaps in order to rid the cabinet of an incubus, he elevated McReynolds to the Supreme Court where for twenty-three years he resisted social progress more bitterly than did even the other conservatives among his brethren.

Wilson had been too casual to avoid the mistake of appointing a man so unrepresentative of his own standards and ideas. When his next chance arose in 1916, after thoughtful consideration he nominated Louis D. Brandeis. It was one of the boldest strokes of his presidency. A radical in the eyes of Bourbon Democrats and Republicans, Brandeis had attacked big business, befriended organized labor, exposed former President Taft as a liar, and revealed J. P. Morgan's beloved New Haven Railroad as inefficient and corrupt. He had also rejected judicial precedent as a sufficient basis for decisions about social policy. Instead his briefs mustered statistics about wages, hours, and working conditions to make the case against judicial nullification of social reform. That "sociological jurisprudence" frightened the legal establishment which opposed his nomination rancorously, as did the rich and the well-born of the eastern seaboard. They were incensed not the least because Brandeis, though a graduate of the Harvard Law

School, was also a Jew, the first of his religion to be nominated to the Supreme Court. From January through May 1916 the struggle over Brandeis' confirmation engaged the Senate Judiciary Committee. Wilson kept out of it until he felt the moment of decision had arrived. He then published a letter noting the importance of the office and praising the qualities of the man, a letter so unequivocal that it made confirmation a party issue. By a strict party vote the committee recommended Brandeis, and with only one Democrat opposed, the Senate approved his appointment.

Frankly delighted, Wilson knew his sponsorship of Brandeis would please the progressives whose votes he wanted that November, but he had a more enduring purpose. "There is probably no more important duty," he had written in his letter of May, "imposed upon the President in connection with the general administration of the Government than that of naming members of the Supreme Court. . . . I named Mr. Brandeis . . . because I knew him to be singularly qualified by learning, by gifts, and by character for the position." So he was, as his long service on the court attested. In risking conservative and anti-Semitic wrath by nominating Brandeis, the President balanced his error in the case of McReynolds. Later in 1916 he filled another vacancy with the appointment of United States District Judge John H. Clarke, a noncontroversial figure who could be relied upon for an enlightened reading of the law.

Still, the error in the case of McReynolds displayed the fallibility of even a wise governor, a president both qualified and eager to lead, and it therefore also exposed the problem of government by experts, even talented but also necessarily fallible experts.

During 1916 Wilson had a sure political touch. He followed his nomination of Brandeis by approving reform measures he had previously opposed, one an act forbidding child labor, another an act establishing a system to provide inexpensive loans to farmers. In a successful effort to put off a national railroad strike, he persuaded Congress to pass a law reducing the hours of work by railroad laborers, and he then permitted an increase in rates to cover the resulting costs. Those achievements strengthened his identification with progressivism, still a formidable spirit in American political life. They allowed him to claim, with some plausibility, that the Democratic party had made the 1912 Progressive platform its own. And they attracted indispensable progressive support to Wilson's candidacy for reelection.

That candidacy also profited from the reorganization of the Democratic National Committee in 1916 and from the breadth of the coalition the party had put together. Less dependent than formerly on the city machines, which in 1916 were still loyal but rather passive, the Democrats had majorities not only in the solid South but now also in the agricultural West and among reform-minded professional men and women. A tenuous combination of those interests, a combination vital for the future of the party, reelected Wilson by a narrow margin. In his first term, he had, like Roosevelt, carried his program in Congress, taken command of his party, and held the country at his side.

In 1916 Wilson's foreign policies counted as much as did domestic issues. Before becoming president, as he admitted, he had given little thought to the conduct of foreign affairs, but he had arrived at some general, imprecise assumptions about the United States in its international setting. Like so many of his countrymen, he believed in the special virtue and mission of the American people, the worthy successors of the early colonists who had fled a corrupt Europe to build a better society, a city on the hill, on an unspoiled continent. Free of an artificial class system, of monarchy and aristocracy, the United States, in that view, stood apart from the network of alliances and the imperial rivalries of the old world. American democratic institutions, flourishing on their own soil, provided a model for other nations, old and new. The beneficence Wilson attributed to the American political system he also attached to the country's economic system. Competitive capitalism, he believed, purged of the excrescences of privilege that his New Freedom attacked, provided unequaled opportunity for the self-advancement of individuals and the creation of national wealth. In that interpretation democracy and capitalism marched hand in hand, and beckoned the world to follow.

Similar assumptions found a variety of expressions in the early twentieth century. Adherents of Theodore Roosevelt's "large view," conservatives like Henry Cabot Lodge and progressives like Albert J. Beveridge, advocated accelerating the destiny of the United States by planting the flag in distant outposts. Those expansionists, enthusiasts for a strong navy, preached an American version of the white man's burden that Wilson had come largely to reject by 1913. In theory at least, he had moved closer to the anti-imperialist school which warned that colonial ventures would corrupt American innocence and destroy the nation's ability to project an image of the good society for emulation elsewhere. The President had also a large sympathy for the legalists, among them William Howard Taft and William Jennings Bryan, who sought to refine and apply a body of international law and a system of international arbitration to govern relations among states and to preserve peace.

In foreign policy, as in domestic, Wilson operated from no fully articulated body of theory. He held fast to only one predicate: "The force of America," he declared in the midst of an early crisis, "is the force of moral principle . . . there is nothing else that she loves, and . . . there is nothing else for which she will contend." Moral principle, as it emerged in his interpretation, entailed a duty to end colonialism both in practice and by example; to fulfill the mission of America by parading the benefits of republican government, democratic elections and competitive markets; and to work for peace through "orderly processes of just government based upon law."

Nowhere did Wilson and Bryan more clearly reveal the honesty and the innocence of those intentions than in Asia. They withdrew the United States from a consortium of Western powers that Taft had joined for the purpose of building a railroad network in China and stabilizing finances there. Opposed to the monopolistic privileges the consortium conferred on a few bankers and to its threat to Chinese sovereignty, Wilson was eager "to help China in some better way." He did so by recognizing the republican government of China established in 1912 by the successful revolution led by Sun Yat-sen. Without prior consultation with interested European states or with Japan, countries which had yet to act, in May 1913 he formally welcomed "the new China . . . into the family of nations" and expressed his "confident hope" for Chinese well-being under "a republican form of government." More than he then realized, the revolution in China had only begun, the republican government had only a tenuous authority, and China remained too weak to protect itself from foreign interference and too poor to resist foreign involvement in its economy. But in acting from principle, the President abandoned no significant American interest.

So, too, he cultivated peace and good will in his relations with Japan. In 1913 a California statute forbade alien ownership of land in that state, a prohibition addressed against Japanese immigrants who were ineligible for citizenship. The President, by no means devoid of racial prejudice himself and cautious about preserving states' rights, attempted to persuade the Californians to use less offensive language than they did. He failed. The Japanese government in May submitted an "urgent and explicit" protest, and in the charged atmosphere of Washington, senior military and naval officers, holding that war was possible, recommended the transfer of gunboats from China to the Philippines to protect those islands. Wilson declined to take that provocative step. When the Joint Board of the Army and Navy protested his decision, he warned that its members had no right to question settled policy and that he would abolish the board if they did so again. To the Japanese government Bryan advised "restraint and calmness" with the reminder that "nothing is final between friends." Though the Japanese remained understandably bitter, the crisis passed. Wilson's diplomacy of friendship had worked at least as well as Roosevelt's earlier show of force, and had wholly avoided an unwarranted and irresponsible stab toward war.

Roosevelt had come to see the vulnerability of the Philippines; Wilson in dealing with those islands became the first statesman of the century to retreat from colonialism. He appointed a governor-general with a mandate to prepare the Philippines for self-government and he influenced the drafting of the Jones bill which Congress passed in 1916. It established a bicameral Philippine legislature elected almost entirely by the Filipinos themselves and endowed with near autonomy over internal affairs. The act also stated that the United States would withdraw after a period of transition assured a stable native government. "A very satisfactory advance," Wilson called the measure, in the "policy of extending . . . genuine self-government."

Yet Wilson's anticolonialism and friendly diplomacy did not solve American problems in Asia. Even if independent, the Philippines would still need American protection against possible Japanese expansion. Even though blessed, as Wilson believed, with at least the semblance of republican institutions, China lacked the means to resist the extraordinary territorial and commercial demands that Japan made in 1915 while the European nations were preoccupied with war. Wilson and Bryan then stated that the United States would not recognize any agreement impairing Chinese territorial integrity, American treaty rights in China, or the open door—the policy of equal access to China of commercial ventures of all national origins. In Wilson's view, republican institutions and a free market were related. His dedication to both led him unrealistically to assume that they fit both Chinese and Filipino culture and deserved American support in those countries, even though the Asian societies did not remotely resemble the United States.

In Latin America his pursuit of those principles produced even more ambiguous results. Though eager to cultivate the friendship of the nations of the Caribbean area, Wilson, like Roosevelt before him, made the autonomy of those nations conditional upon "orderly processes of just government based upon law." Though the President disavowed the commercialism of Taft's "dollar diplomacy," he allowed Bryan to rely on American bankers and their agents to underwrite loans and to supervise their collection in small Caribbean states still bankrupt, underdeveloped, and only superficially republican. Their predictable financial and political misfortunes led Wilson to establish American protectorates in Santo Domingo and Haiti, and to sustain an authoritarian regime in Nicaragua.

Developments in Mexico especially revealed the uncertain consequences of Wilson's motives, as well as the possibilities that exclusively presidential initiatives could pull the nation toward war. In February 1913 a reactionary coup d'état led by General Victoriano Huerta overthrew the two-year-old revolutionary government. The forces of revolution, the Constitutionalists, continued their fight under their implacable leader, Venustiano Carranza. Sympathetic to the revolution and unmoved by Americans with financial interests in Mexico, Wilson refused to send an ambassador to Huerta's "government of assassins." In October Huerta, supported by British oil interests, made himself military dictator. Wilson then demanded Huerta's retirement by "such means as may be necessary." The United States, he said, would never again seek land by conquest, but he proposed to sponsor "constitutional liberty" in Mexico and so to advance the world toward "those great heights where there shines unobstructed the light of the justice of God." As he put it privately, he would "teach the South American republicans to elect good men."

To that end Wilson induced the British in March 1914 to

withdraw their recognition of Huerta by promising them protection for British property in the event of a Constitutionalist victory. He tried to cover that incautious promise by proposing to Carranza that the United States would join him in a war against Huerta if he would keep the revolution orderly. Opposed to American intervention for any reason, Carranza refused. But he needed American arms. The Constitutionalists, he said, would respect the rights of property if Wilson lifted the embargo on shipments of arms to Mexico. Wilson did so.

The President also found an excuse to intervene. In April an Huertista colonel arrested some American sailors who had gone ashore in Tampico. Though the local commanding general apologized, he would not order a twenty-one gun salute to the American flag. On that petty pretext, Wilson prepared plans to occupy Vera Cruz, Mexico's most important Caribbean port, and asked Congress for authority to use force to obtain from Huerta "the fullest recognition of the rights and dignity of the United States." Before Congress had time to act, Wilson ordered the navy to seize Vera Cruz in order to prevent a German ship from landing arms for Huerta. He also directed his military staff to work on plans for all-out war.

Mediation by Argentina, Brazil and Chile defused that crisis, though Wilson continued to insist both on the removal of Huerta and on "necessary agrarian and political reforms" in Mexico. It was Carranza who accomplished those objectives. Yet Wilson began to plot the overthrow of Carranza in connivance with Pancho Villa, an ambitious rascal who had deserted the Constitutionalists to lead a personal movement of his own. During 1915 Villa's guerrillas retreated to northern Mexico while the revolution, now in a stage of terror, exploded at times in episodes involving the destruction of private property and physical violence against Roman Catholic priests and nuns. American jingoes, Theodore Roosevelt at the fore, demanded direct intervention, which Wilson sturdily resisted. Engaged in sensitive negotiations with Germany, he also realized he could not divert the revolu-

tion from its course. In October he extended *de facto* recognition
to the Carranza regime. But Villa, incensed by that decision and
eager to harass Carranza by provoking the United States, murdered a group of Americans in Mexico in January 1916, and two
months later brashly raided a town in New Mexico. Wilson then
sent a punitive expedition across the border where it failed to
catch Villa but twice engaged in skirmishes with Constitutionalist
forces. The President went so far as to call up the National Guard
before Carranza, burdened with domestic problems, and Wilson,
enmeshed in the diplomacy of the war in Europe, put aside their
differences by referring them to a joint commission. The American troops left Mexico in January 1917, and in March Wilson
granted Carranza *de jure* recognition.

For four years Wilson had struggled to accommodate his sense of
principle to the revolutionary conditions in Mexico. Though he
avoided war, he brought the country close to it, and he trapped
himself in messy military engagements that violated Mexican
sovereignty. Wilson had tripped over his own progressive assumptions. There was no way to reconcile popular government
in Mexico with the election of a neutral elite committed to gradual change. There was no such elite, no body of technicians who
could mediate among social groups of differing interests. Indeed
in Mexico there remained no room for mediation. Social conditions had come to demand the kind of radical solutions and attendant political violence that alarmed American reformers in their
own country. Roosevelt, as he boasted, would have crushed the
Mexicans underfoot. Wilson exercised more restraint but nevertheless infuriated them. His faith, the faith of American reformers in orderly progress under law, faltered in the face of revolution. So confronted, at least at Vera Cruz and in his relations
with Villa, he had compromised principle to expediency; he had
clothed the art of persuasion in the armor of repression.

The great war that broke out in Europe in 1914 challenged the
assumptions of liberals everywhere about the capacity of law and

reason to guide the affairs of man. That war grew out of the rivalries of the major powers for territory, prestige, and trade, and out of the resulting jealousies and suspicions. It pitted against each other two alliances—one of Great Britain, France, and Russia, later joined by Italy as well as China and Japan; the other of Germany, Austria-Hungary and Turkey. Though the war had been brewing for over a decade, the beginning of hostilities caught almost all Americans, including Wilson, surprised and unprepared. They did not and could not yet understand the horror of modern warfare, nor could they foresee the enormous impact of the war on the United States or the grave problems of policy that impact would create.

The United States, Wilson declared when the war began, would "speak the counsels of peace and accommodation" and play "a part of impartial mediation." He urged Americans to be "neutral in fact as well as in name . . . impartial in thought as well as in action." As innocent as they were noble, those expressions did not anticipate the saturnalia of emotions the war would breed. Once the ghastly slaughter had begun, once mutual suspicion had become mutual hatred, no belligerent was willing to accept mediation except to gain terms equivalent to victory. Within the United States there could be no neutrality of thought. Millions of first and second generation immigrants retained some sense of identification with their homelands. With exceptions of course, German-Americans sympathized with the Central powers, as did Irish-Americans who detested England; most other large immigrant groups sided with the Allies. Apart from the Anglophilia endemic throughout the East Coast, the German invasion of Belgium in 1914 in direct violation of a treaty between the two nations—a "scrap of paper" the Germans called it—offended many Americans. Then and thereafter British and German propaganda served to intensify the attitudes of thousands eager to have their prejudices confirmed.

Partiality of thought compromised Wilson's plea for neutrality far less than did his own policies. Distinct advantages for the Western powers flowed from his interpretation of the rights and duties of a neutral nation, an interpretation grounded in "the existing rules of international law" as he and his counselors understood them. On that basis the President insisted upon the American right to trade with the belligerents. Since Great Britain controlled the sea ways, that trade gave the Western powers alone access to American raw materials and manufactories essential to their arsenals. Wilson made no deliberate decision either to penalize Germany or to stimulate the American economy by permitting French and British purchases. Rather, without predicting the consequences of his policy, which would have been a large order, he characteristically stood by the law—the rules of neutrality that required access by belligerents to American markets. That course was congruent with his deference, in domestic policy, to judicial readings of constitutional law. In 1914 Congress expressed no objection to his stance, though Congress, of course, had no more foresight than did the President, no more insight into the ways in which a continuing defense of neutral rights and duties could lead to belligerency. If in 1914 Wilson had asked for a general embargo, Congress would certainly not have approved of one, and the imposition of an embargo would in itself have been prejudicial to the Allies.

Wilson protested continually and emphatically against the operation of the blockade of Germany that the British instituted. They narrowly limited the kinds of goods American vessels could carry to neutral European ports from which transshipments could reach Germany. They diverted suspect shipping to British ports, confiscated many cargoes, interfered with American mails, and blacklisted American firms for violating their rules. Those practices incontestably infringed upon neutral rights. Though Wilson's resulting protests annoyed the British, they had thought through the consequences of their policy before they applied it. Resolved "to secure the maximum of blockade that could be enforced without a rupture with the United States" and dependent upon American supplies, they yielded enough to Wilson to keep him talking, albeit irritably. Since they allowed no cotton shipments to Germany, at his request they even furnished funds to stabilize cotton prices at a level satisfactory to the American South. For his part, again within the letter of international law, Wilson permitted American bankers to make the loans without which the British and French could not have sustained their volume of purchases in the United States. Again, too, he failed to foresee that the American stake in an Allied victory would therefore grow.

That stake did not force the United States into belligerency, though the loans, as Bryan said, violated "the true spirit of neutrality." The drift toward war arose principally from the problems presented by the German submarines, Wilson's reactions to them, and the calculated German responses to him. Unable to penetrate the British blockade, the Germans attempted to cut off supplies to England and France by sending U-boats into the Atlantic to seek out and destroy Allied shipping. Submarines, then novel as well as deadly weapons, could not conform to the conventional rules for cruiser warfare. Those rules required commerce destroyers, before attacking merchantmen, to warn their targets and then to make a reasonable effort to save the lives of passengers and crew. But submarines depended upon surprise for their effectiveness, were vulnerable to gunfire when they surfaced, and had no room to carry survivors of a sinking ship.

From first to last, Wilson stood by the conventional rules for cruiser warfare. In February 1915 Germany proclaimed a war zone around the British Isles and warned that enemy ships in that area would be sunk on sight and neutral ships endangered because of British misuse of neutral flags. Wilson told the British not to use the stars and stripes. In a sharper note to Germany, he called the sinking of merchantmen without visit and search "a wanton act" and declared that the United States would regard the destruction of American ships or American lives on belligerent ships as a "flagrant violation of neutral rights" for which he would hold Germany to a "strict accountability."

That strong vocabulary vested traditional American interpretations of neutral rights with a new urgency. In the absence of congressional instruction to the contrary, the President, according to the recognized responsibilities of his office, had now to apply his interpretation of the issue in specific instances as they arose. In so doing, in spite of his passionate desire for peace, he risked raising questions of national grandeur and of moral absolutes that would much reduce, perhaps even eliminate, a cool congressional reconsideration of the principles he had announced.

The first major confrontation over submarines occurred in May 1915 with the sinking of the British passenger liner *Lusitania*. Hundreds of men, women and children, many of them Americans, went down with the ship. Those deaths stunned the American people. Theodore Roosevelt, the voice of the militants, accused Germany of "piracy" and "murder" and advocated the immediate severance of diplomatic relations. Americans sympathetic to Germany or opposed to any step toward war advocated arbitration and even a prohibition of travel aboard belligerent ships. The weight of opinion stood for a middle course that would provide some redress without forsaking neutrality. That was Wilson's purpose. Most public men who wrote him appealed for peace, and Democratic leaders in Congress advised him that the country did not want war and Congress would not declare it. He addressed the Germans firmly. He brushed aside as a secondary issue their argument excusing the sinking because the *Lusitania* had carried ammunition. The United States, he said, was contending for "something much greater than mere rights of property," for "nothing less high and sacred than the rights of humanity." The rachet of his rhetoric lifted his view of international law to a celestial plane. "Illegal and inhuman acts," he wrote, were "manifestly indefensible," especially when they deprived neutrals of their "acknowledged rights," even "the right to life it-self." Requesting both an apology and reparations, the President observed again that submarines could not operate against un-armed merchantmen without violating "many sacred principles of justice and humanity." Virtually, then, he was demanding crippling restrictions on their use.

Though Wilson's words burdened negotiations with metaphys-ical imperatives of questionable relevance, he settled with relief for moderate terms. Germany would not admit the illegality of sinking the *Lusitania* or of any other sinking. Still, the Imperial Government expressed regret over the loss of American lives, for which it offered an indemnity. It also promised not to sink pas-senger liners without warning provided they did not try to escape or resist. It could do no more, it said, without giving up subma-rines. That satisfied Wilson, as it did most Americans, who agreed with him that they desired only "peace with honor."

In private Wilson cherished a larger purpose. "It would look," he had written in August, 1915 to the woman he was about to marry, "as if Europe had finally determined to commit suicide . . . and the only way we can hope to save it is by changing the course of its thoughts. That's the only reason it's worth-while to write Notes to Germany or England or anybody else. They alter no facts; they change no plans or purposes; they accomplish noth-ing immediate; but they *may* convey thoughts that will, if only unconsciously, affect opinion, and set up a counter current. At least such is my hope; and it is also the only hope for those dis-tracted English." Obviously his hope was to save England but also Europe. He endeavored to achieve it not by notes alone but also by continually pressing the belligerents for an armistice. Still, whatever his private thoughts, in his notes to Germany his invocations of honor and of the sacred principles of humanity left him with diminished room for future concessions.

He tried to eliminate the problem by pressing the Western powers to cease arming merchant vessels. That solution would have delighted the Germans who could then have warned or even visited Allied ships before destroying them and their important cargoes. Predictably Great Britain rejected Wilson's rather naïve proposal. He then backed away and reasserted his adherence to the old rules for cruiser warfare. Now Bryan, LaFollette, and their like-minded friends in Congress, some of them ready to support an embargo to prevent the war they saw just ahead, found a "moral treason" in letting American citizens continue to provoke ominous crises by traveling on vulnerable belligerent ships. Resolutions introduced in Congress to prevent that controversial travel pushed Wilson once again to link law and national grandeur. "Once accept a single abatement of right," he told Congress in opposing the resolutions, "and many other humiliations would follow, and the whole fine fabric of international law might crumble under our hands." Apart from that domino theory of neutral rights, Wilson held that the nation's "honor and self-respect" were involved: "We covet peace and shall preserve it at any cost but the loss of honor." A sufficient number of rebellious Democrats yielded to the President to secure a vote to table the resolutions.

It was the Germans, not Wilson, who temporarily rescued his policy. In March 1916 a German submarine, without warning, torpedoed the unarmed French channel steamer *Sussex* with eight resulting casualties. Wilson in April informed Congress that it had become "painfully evident" that his initial assertion of 1915 was true, submarine warfare was inevitably "incompatible with the principles of humanity, the long established and incontrovertible rights of neutrals, and the sacred immunities of noncombatants." Unless Germany abandoned submarine warfare against passenger liners and merchant vessels, the United States would break off diplomatic relations. The Germans then beat a calculated retreat. Because they lacked the submarines to maintain a useful blockade of the British Isles, the Kaiser's council in May 1916 decided temporarily to placate the United States. They agreed that submarines would thereafter observe the rules of visit and search, but they also warned that they would reverse that decision unless the United States compelled Great Britain also to obey international law. Ignoring that condition, Wilson accepted the German assurances.

Again most Americans rejoiced. With the "*Sussex* pledge," Wilson appeared to have preserved both peace and honor. As the German government and the President both realized, any reckless German U-boat captain could fire the torpedo that would dissolve that fantasy. Wilson was disingenuous in permitting his party to pitch the campaign of 1916 on the note of peace. He did not invent the party's slogan, "He kept us out of war," which applied to Mexico as well as to Germany; but neither did he repudiate its implication that he could continue to. The peace issue contributed as much as any other to his victory.

In order to keep the implicit promise and to end the "war of exhaustion and attrition," Wilson attempted to mediate between the belligerents. He was ready, he said, to pledge the "whole force" of the United States to enforce peace and future security. He intended to ask each side for a definition of the guarantees and objectives for which it was fighting and then to direct American policy, short of war, to assist whichever party proved disposed to settle more reasonably. He had yet to act when Germany in December 1916 announced its willingness to negotiate. Wilson then moved as he had planned to, but no government would reply to his request for a definition of purpose. The Germans called for a conference among belligerents, a course the Allies rejected, demanding instead indemnities from Germany and the destruction of her power. Privately the British assured Wilson they would discuss peace if German terms were reasonable. But in January 1917 the Germans put forward draconian terms tantamount to an Allied surrender. The Germans expected cessions of territory in Africa, along the Baltic, and from Belgium, Luxembourg, and France. The Chancellor and his associates who had earlier approved the *Sussex* pledge for tactical reasons now also accepted the military decision, which they announced, to resume unrestricted submarine warfare. They believed they had built enough submarines to blockade the British Isles and to destroy American ships and shipments. A rupture with the United States, they concluded, mattered less than the quick advantage they predicted from the success of the U-boats.

Genuinely dismayed, Wilson in a major address spoke, he said, for "the silent mass of mankind." In the name of "the revelation of our Lord and Savior . . . [that] wars will never have an ending until men cease to hate," he proposed immediate peace, a league of nations to preserve it, a "peace without victory," a "peace among equals." His message of Christian hope was as futile as it was heady. Though he did not break relations with Germany or hasten military preparations, he asked Congress for explicit authority to arm American merchant vessels and to take other measures to protect American ships and citizens at sea. To muster votes for that bill, he also released a secret German note, earlier intercepted and reported by the British, instructing the German minister in Mexico, in the event of war with the United States, to suggest that Mexico join Germany and invite Japan to do so, too. In spite of the ensuing wave of anger in the United States, the House passed a bill giving Wilson only the authority to arm merchantmen, and in the Senate a dozen antiwar progressives talked a stronger bill to death.

Furious with that "little group of willful men," Wilson on his own authority as commander in chief ordered the merchant ships armed. Few guns were yet in place on March 18, 1917, when German submarines sank three American ships without warning. At that juncture the first revolution in Russia established a limited monarchy that ended the Czarist despotism which many Americans resented. That development made it easier to join cause with the Russians. Further, Wilson learned from the British that they could not go on without American men, money, and supplies. The concatenation of events persuaded the President and his whole cabinet to decide for war. Racked by that decision, Wilson confided in a friendly journalist: "He said war would overturn the world we had known . . . that there would be a dictated peace, a victorious peace. . . . He said . . . war . . . required illiberalism at home . . . the spirit of ruthless brutality . . ." He could see no alternative.

In that pass Wilson had to convince himself, as well as Congress and the American people, that the nobility of their purpose justified the terrible ordeal they faced. Germany had to represent autocracy and evil. "The world," the President said in his message of April 2, 1917, to the special session of Congress he had convened, "must be made safe for democracy. Its peace must be planted upon the tested foundations of political liberty. . . . We are but one of the champions of the rights of mankind. . . . It is a fearful thing to lead this great people into war. . . . But the right is more precious than peace, and we shall fight for the things we have always carried nearest our hearts,—for democracy . . . for the rights and liberties of small nations, for a universal dominion of right by such a concert of free peoples as shall bring peace and safety to all nations and make the world itself at last free."

That deluded and delusive peroration hid the actualities of Allied intentions, about which Wilson was amply informed. It raised expectations for the peace that no war and no statesman could satify. Though it helped to sustain brave men and women during the months ahead, it spared those who fought none of the fear and anger of their experience. Yet when he spoke as he did, Wilson surely believed what he said. He had to in order to escape the now palpable conflict between his earnest hopes for peace and his fervent commitment to neutral rights. The former had required a practical resilience that the latter impeded, particularly because human rights did not so neatly correspond to neutral rights as Wilson maintained. As it worked out, Wilson's formulation perhaps counted less in the end than did German intransigence, but his formulation did matter. He conditioned Americans to accept war on the basis of national honor and moral purpose. He bent the Congress toward the lines of his policy on the same basis. His first response to the blockade the Germans announced in 1915 rested upon assumptions he never relinquished. Recast and inflated, those assumptions led Wilson to rest his primary case for war not on law or even national interest or honor, but on transcendental propositions in which he enveloped them all.

The confusion was not peculiarly Wilson's. Most American reformers of his time, like most other Americans, were loath to ask themselves fundamental questions. They fell back instead on moral assertions. The meliorists who made an operable case for continual advances in government regulation of business ordinarily hesitated to question the relevance of capitalism in any form as an economic system. By and large, they simply dismissed socialism as a dirty abomination. As one consequence they talked constantly not about systems but about morality. The resulting ambiguities eased the processes of politics by obfuscating important, though divisive, issues. Similarly Wilson and most of his contemporaries did not ask themselves whether international law was relevant to modern warfare or, more profoundly, whether modern warfare—revealed at its most horrid on the western front—constituted a tolerable instrument of national policy. Rather, they defended international law as a shield against reality, though partly also to serve commercial advantage, and they aggrandized that law by identifying it with the rights of man and the reputation of their country. They continued to do so even after their international politics failed in the most essential of political functions, the peaceful reconciliation of conflicting purposes. Even if they had asked the fundamental questions, their answers would probably have been the same, but their discourse would have been more precise, less clouded by moralistic ambiguities. As it was, unrecognized and unacknowledged confusions gave rise to the apocalyptical message that Wilson delivered to his national audience, largely a cheering audience, in April 1917.

Wilson's policies for the wartime home front displayed the ambiguities inherent in progressive thinking more starkly than ever before. The exigencies of mobilization, for which the United States had not been prepared, impelled the President to create a number of powerful war agencies, all located within his expanded executive office. Each of them exercised more authority within its assigned sphere than had any pre-existent federal administrative body. The War Industries Board, responsible for managing war production and for allocation of industrial materials, gathered some hundred businessmen, the obvious experts, to discharge its duties. On the whole able and patriotic executives, they nevertheless remained as much the representatives of private industry and its interests as were the bankers earlier recruited to the Federal Reserve Board. There was nothing corrupt in that representation, but it was not politically neutral. So, too, the Food Administration permitted a substantial increase in wholesale grain and meat prices to encourage more production. Though western farmers would like to have earned even larger profits, they had a concerned friend in Herbert C. Hoover, the head of the administration, who in the private opinion of one observer counted hogs in his sleep. With its subsidiaries, the War Labor Administration ran an effective conciliation service, standardized wages and hours in industries engaged in war work, and registered and placed millions of men and women in that work. In spite of the agency's efforts, millions of workers went on strike to obtain more pay. Their successes, along with the work of the WLA, resulted in a seventy percent increase in real wages, and business profits rose some thirty percent.

The federal bureaucracies that exercised the mediating authority in the wartime economy served the interest of industry, labor, and agriculture, as the advocates of reform through rationalization had believed they could. In the process the government grew in size and power. But the agencies did not subdue the conflicts among major interest groups, nor did they operate according to peculiary expert or scientific principles. With exceptions—the Railroad Administration and the Fuel Administration were two—the wartime agencies represented their own constituencies whose needs continued to conflict. The reconciliation of those conflicts through administrative rulings bought cooperation at the price of favor, kept the machinery of war whirling, but charged the costs in the form of accelerating inflation to unrepresented individuals.

The structure of wartime government provided an antecedent pattern for the contemporary state, but the use of government also forboded the corruption of that state. Just as Wilson had predicted, illiberalism and brutality imbued the wartime mood. One of his agencies, the Committee on Public Information, generated a propaganda of hatred of all things German, a propaganda with overtones condemning all forms of dissent. The President signed the Espionage Act of 1917 and the Sedition Act of 1918 under which the Justice Department prosecuted Americans for criticizing the Red Cross, or the YMCA, or the methods of financing the war. In the latter statute Congress allowed for the punishment of expressions of opinion which, regardless of their probable consequences, were "disloyal, profane, scurrilous or abusive" of the American form of government, flag or uniform. Though the United States was never in danger of invasion or even attack, though instances of sabotage were remarkably few, the executive departments used their authority to close the mail to pacifist or socialist publications; to deny freedom of speech to voluble but innocuous radicals; to imprison Eugene V. Debs, the head of the Socialist party, for opposing the war; to persecute labor radicals; and in the immediate aftermath of war, to harass and detain immigrants guilty of nothing but a foreign birth. Public passions, private vigilante groups, congressional recklessness, and judicial timidity contributed to the indiscriminate violations of civil liberties which several of the President's appointees encouraged and Wilson did nothing to prevent.

Wilson and many of his associates had, of course, been progressive, as had Theodore Roosevelt and others like him who advocated even harsher repression. They had shared a view of society and a confidence in gradual reform that depended for realization on their assumptions about the basic decency and self-restraint of the American people and their elected leaders. Implicit in those assumptions lay a trust in the usefulness of a free exchange of ideas. Now, during a struggle defined as a war to make the world safe for democracy—the kind of democracy they said they cherished—many progressives unhesitatingly met dissent, violent or peaceful, with suppression. So did most conservatives, but they had never pretended to a faith either in social reform or majoritarian government. In the name of republican institutions, the Wilson administration violated the Constitution; in the name of law, it allowed license; in the name of democracy, it practiced autocracy. Those wartime misadventures disheartened the reflective reformers who had not earlier examined the contradictions generic to their own hopes and beliefs. They had now to doubt the reasonableness of a majority, the reliability of a trained elite, the neutrality and beneficence of strong government.

Wilson yielded to the illiberalism he forecast partly because he suffered any expedient that seemed to him necessary to materialize his vision of a liberal and enduring peace. He could sustain that vision only by hoping to supersede the punitive designs incorporated in the secret treaties among the Allies. By his choice the United States, affirming its mythical innocence, fought not as an Allied nation but as an associated belligerent, with the others but not of them. So insulated, Wilson announced the particulars of his purpose. The occasion for his celebrated address to Congress of January 1918 arose following the Bolshevik revolution in Russia the previous November. Lenin and his forces, after seizing control of the government, began to negotiate a separate peace with Germany, and in order to embarrass the Allies, released the terms of the secret treaties they found among the Czar's records. In rebuttal the British Prime Minister, disingenuously as it developed, and the American President, naïvely but sincerely, asserted their commitment to a just peace.

"We demand," Wilson said in his address, "that the world be made . . . safe . . . against force and selfish aggression." He then laid out his Fourteen Points. Five were general: an end to secret agreements; free use of the seas in war and peace; the reduction of armaments; the removal of barriers to trade; an impartial adjustment of colonial claims. Eight points pertained to territorial settlements in Europe according to the principle of self-determination. The fourteenth climactic point proposed "a general association of nations . . . under specific covenants for the purpose of affording mutual guarantees of political independence and territorial integrity to great and small states alike."

The Fourteen Points gave a global application to Wilson's moral principles. In keeping with them, he followed his impulse to make guilt personal. He intended to punish not the German people, only the Kaiser, and to begin the redemption of Germany by eliminating monarchy there. His terms reflected familiar American, particularly Wilsonian goals: support for the independence of emerging nations, for republican institutions within them and elsewhere, for a universal open door to commercial enterprise, for freedom of the seas to freight that commerce. Whether moral or not, those objectives were distinctly political, and advantageous to the United States. They were also only partly official, not yet the settled policy of the Congress where protectionists still opposed free trade and isolationists any continuing entanglement with Europe. They were, too, by no means binding on the Allied governments which had had no part in their formulation and little taste for certain of their implications.

Yet Wilson made small allowance for the politics of attaining his terms. He did not try to make American participation in the war contingent upon Allied modification of the secret treaties. He did not consult his political adversaries in Congress. On the contrary, during the congressional campaigns of 1918 he cultivated partisanship. His party, as he knew, had been weakened by the disenchantment of western farmers over larger favors rendered to cotton rather than grain crops, the resentment of former eastern progressives over high income taxes, the disgruntlement of the city machines and their Democratic constituents over the incipient national prohibition of the manufacture and sale of alcoholic beverages. Instead of addressing those issues, Wilson appealed to the electorate to vote Democratic "if you have approved of my leadership and wish me to continue to be your unembarrassed spokesman in affairs at home and abroad." Then negotiating an armistice with Germany, and on the verge of negotiating a peace, he said the return of a Republican majority would "certainly be interpreted on the other side of the water as a repudiation of my leadership." Furious with Wilson's tone and victorious in the elections in which they carried both houses of Congress, the Republicans thereafter claimed that foreign policy had determined the results.

Many Republicans, speaking for many Americans of both parties, had consistently attacked Wilson's "peace without victory." They wanted to march to Berlin, hang the Kaiser, and demand unconditional surrender. They were dissatisfied with Wilson's tough armistice which he delayed until he had forced the abdication of the Kaiser and which he designed so as to prevent Germany from resuming the war. It was also a reasonable armistice, based, with the tentative and reluctant approval of the Allies, on the Fourteen Points. But after the election the President had no mandate for those points at home, and only conditional acceptance of them from the Allies. Nevertheless he appointed to the American Peace Commission, which he decided to head himself, only men sympathetic to his purpose and no Republican of standing in his party or in the Senate. Then, acclaimed as a savior by crowds in England, France, and Italy, he assumed a savior's stance. He embodied, he believed, the spirit of a great nation. Though other nations shared that spirit, their leaders did not represent them. So it fell to the Americans, "the only disinterested people," and it fell directly to him, to instill "a great triumph of the right" in the treaty which the victors were to write at Paris.

Wilson realized that the proceedings there would result in some departures from the Fourteen Points on various geographic, ethnographic, and military issues. Yet he expected "the individual items of the settlement" to be "altogether satisfactory." More important, he counted on the deliberations of the future League of Nations to serve permanently "the interests of peace and justice." The establishment of the League, his primary objective, would organize "the moral force of the world."

That prospect caught the imagination of millions of Europeans and Americans, but Wilson underestimated, as did many of his admirers, the obstacles, some of his own making, that stood in his way. The great war had depleted the human and physical resources of every European power. It had precipitated the collapse of Austria-Hungary where the peoples of east central Europe were bent upon creating their own nations, whatever the decisions of the conference at Paris. The infant German republic suffered a shortage of food because of the continuing Allied blockade and faced revolution in its eastern reaches where Bolshevik influence and terror had spread. Indeed Bolshevism, feeding on the devastation the war had left, was advancing in Eastern Europe and triumphant in Russia where only pockets of resistance remained. Frightened by those developments, the Allied leaders excluded Russia, which had earlier capitulated to Germany, from the peace table. Wilson, a partner to that decision, also ordered American troops to Siberia to join a futile Allied effort to support counterrevolutionaries there.

With revolution ebullient, Eastern Europe in turmoil, Germany sullen, and Allied forces in command of the territories their various nations coveted, Wilson had little chance to organize the political, much less the moral force of the world. He did contribute magnificently to that purpose. He made the League of Nations an integral part of the treaty. He blocked the outright accession by the Allies of Germany's former colonies by devising the mandate system. Though the British and Japanese received immediate control over colonies their troops already held, their control was subjected, according to the terms of the treaty, to supervision of the League and defined to obligate the preparation of indigenous peoples for independence. Wilson also prevented the permanent German loss of the Saar basin to France and of Silesia to Poland. The treaty stipulated that, after a period of occupation, plebiscites conducted by the League would determine the national affiliation of those areas.

The President had also to make substantial concessions. The Japanese acquired more former German holdings in China than many Americans considered reasonable. The French moderated their demands only after Wilson agreed to a security treaty that guaranteed American and British assistance in the event of a future German attack, a treaty that had small chance of approval in the Senate. The Italians obtained a new northern frontier that left thousands of Austrians under their rule and, unavoidably, geographic and military considerations produced other European boundaries that violated the principle of self-determination and rankled local patriots whose hopes were thwarted. In those and other cases, the American kin of the offended folk blamed Wilson, though the fault was rarely his. In the worst solution reached at Paris, he bowed to French and British demands for enormous reparations from Germany. He would have conceded less had it not been for the necessity to renegotiate details of the Covenant of the League in order to mollify the more moderate of the Republican opponents of both League and treaty.

The total product of the conference, the Treaty of Versailles, was probably as satisfactory as any Wilson could have arranged. In his absence it would have been brutal. On Germany, as he said, it was "severe," but much less so than Germany had been to Russia. Except on reparations, it conformed to the spirit, though not to the letter of the Fourteen Points. Most significantly for Wilson, it included the League of Nations and made the League indispensable for working out its provisions. They promised a world order based upon the cooperative deliberations and policies of the developed nations of the West rather than the balance of power which the alliances had proved unable to maintain. The League and all it implied constituted "the main object of the peace," Wilson maintained, ". . . the hope of the world." Yet that outcome was exactly what enough Republican senators to defeat the treaty had warned him not to reach.

At Paris Wilson had brought a new magnificence to the presidency. The first president to go to Europe during his time in office, he had dealt directly with other heads of major governments during the most important and spectacular international conference in more than a century, put a visible American stamp on negotiations, and won agreement to an international organization without precedent. He had become the most renowned statesman in the world.

He had also aroused a dangerous opposition within the United States from large numbers of foreign-born Americans who found something in his treaty they disliked, from isolationists alarmed by the League, from racists on the West Coast who saw the yellow peril in every Japanese gain, and from jealous Republicans determined to republicanize Wilson's work. Many of his former idealistic champions now considered the treaty tainted by compromise and worse than none at all.

Those moods required the delicate political touch the President had employed in 1913–14. In 1919, in contrast, Wilson spurned the spirit and tools of conciliation. He would condone no conditions for senatorial approval of the treaty except the cosmetic explanations he wrote himself. He would not meet even the more moderate Republicans part way. He insisted, in spite of the contrary opinion of the British, the French and his own State Department, that ratification of the treaty with reservations or interpretations would necessitate its renegotiation. He bitterly opposed the particular reservations the Republican leadership proposed, especially one pertaining to Article X of the Covenant of the League, which he had drafted. That article bound signatories "to respect and preserve against external aggression the territorial integrity and . . . political independence of all . . . members of the League." The council of the League, a quasi-executive body composed largely of representatives of the major powers, was to advise members, in the event of aggression, about the means to satisfy that obligation. The Republican reservation asserted that the United States had no obligation to act unless Congress voted to do so. Wilson called that reservation unnecessary and unworthy. Article X, he argued, was permissive. It placed no restraint on the constitutional authority of Congress to declare war or appropriate money. Rather, like the League itself, the article placed a moral duty on signatories of the treaty to share responsibility for preserving peace. Doubtless correct in spirit, that interpretation had little practical meaning. In the event of a test of Article X, with or without the reservation the Senate was debating, Congress did have the power to declare war, but the president had the means, as Wilson had demonstrated between 1914 and 1917 in dealing with Mexico and with Germany, to leave Congress with virtually no tolerable choice. The sponsors of the reservation may have been mean and partisan men, as Wilson believed, but they were also trying to protect the Congress and the nation against a future initiative by the president in cooperation with the League that could make war a *fait accompli*.

Wrapped in a mantle of self-righteousness, Wilson could see

neither the complexities of the issue nor the folly of his rigidity. On a tour of the West to rouse public opinion for his treaty, he stressed the necessity for the League and Article X. Further, he said, "America . . . is the only national idealistic force in the world, and idealism is going to save the world. . . . That is the program of civilization." It was not then the program of the Senate. The victim of a stroke suffered during his tour, Wilson returned to the White House and there to another, crippling stroke, to weeks of incapacity and months of a slow and incomplete recovery. While he was ill, the Senate rejected the treaty, as it did again several months later when he still refused to compromise. In 1920 the Democrats repudiated Wilson by selecting a candidate unidentified with his administration, and the country repudiated both the President and his party by electing the Republicans in a landslide.

Neither the Senate nor the American people were yet ready to save the world in Wilson's way. Even if the United States had ratified the treaty, the League would probably have become, as it did, an instrument to preserve the status quo. Nevertheless the rejection of the treaty, though partly the President's fault, made a travesty of his glorious dream. In spite of his quixotic and refractory behavior, he was leading the nation and the world in the right direction.

Of course the election of 1920 turned on many issues, not just the treaty, but its results also marked the end to progressivism as the robust force in American politics that it had been for almost two decades. The impulse for reform survived, as did scores of the men and women who had nurtured it, but the next significant victories for liberal reform came in a time and under conditions unlike those in which the generation of Theodore Roosevelt and Woodrow Wilson had lived and their kind of meliorism had flourished. The ambiguities of reform also persisted, some of them increasingly blatant as avowed reactionaries gained control of the political and regulatory apparatus the progressives had created.

The election of 1920 marked, too, a temporary eclipse of the presidency. No one of Wilson's three successors viewed the office as he and Roosevelt had. No one of them had serious doubts about the benignity of corporations, or a serious interest in the federal promotion of social equity. No one of them achieved a significant command of his party or of Congress. No one of them sought or attained an important stature in the world. In the absence of a strong president, of a powerful leader resolved to lead, federal public policy drifted, as it had in the last several decades of the nineteenth century, and the federal government atrophied.

To that development Wilson had contributed by insisting upon an unambiguous decision about the Treaty of Versailles. Both he and Roosevelt had won their victories in politics by ignoring or allowing or sometimes even cultivating ambiguities in their policies. Neither most Americans nor most of their political representatives wanted to choose baldly between the myth of a bucolic past and the comforts of an industrial present, between popular elections and elite governance, between equity and efficiency, between national grandeur and national isolation. The President, steward of the people, had to be ambiguous if he was to represent the bulk of his constituency. The great majority of that constituency, eager though many of them were for specific improvements in their own circumstances, believed in republican government, conventional institutions, and a capitalistic economy in which corporations thrived. The great majority accepted the American system, indeed revered it even when they wanted to improve it, and certainly wanted to preserve it. Consequently the ambiguities of reform made them comfortable, just as open and radical criticism made them tense. Two strong presidents succeeded when they served as champions of gradual reform designed to preserve the basic system. Still, their policies, domestic and international, revealed the risks as well as the advantages of their use of their office. Their achievements exposed the contradictions as well as the benefits embedded in their purpose.

3

Franklin Roosevelt and the Problem of Priorities

THE TIMBRE OF THE CONFIDENT VOICE, the determined words it carried across the ether to millions of listening Americans, the hope that it expressed and that its audiences needed, made the inaugural message of Franklin D. Roosevelt as inspiriting as its content was predictive. He had already, in accepting his nomination, pledged himself to a "new deal" for a nation burdened with the worst depression in its history. His campaign speeches, addresses in the progressive tradition, had pointed to his attachment to social and economic reform, specifically to the obligations of the government to open to "everyone an avenue to possess himself of a portion of . . . plenty sufficient for his needs, through his own work," to "assist the development of . . . an economic . . .

order," and to relieve the human suffering and "dire need" afflicting perhaps a fourth or a fifth of all Americans. Now, standing in a drizzle as gray as the prevailing mood on that fourth day of March 1933, the President addressed himself with "candor and . . . decision" to the situation of the country:

Only a foolish optimism can deny the dark realities of the moment. . . . Values have shrunken to fantastic levels . . . the means of exchange are frozen in the currents of trade; the withered leaves of individual enterprise lie on every side; farmers find no markets for their produce; the savings of many years in thousands of families are gone. . . . A host of unemployed . . . face the grim problem of existence . . .

The blame, the President went on, fell upon the managers of industry and finance who had so blithely assumed credit for the high prosperity of the decade preceding the crash of 1929. "Rulers of the exchange of mankind's goods have failed through their own stubbornness and their own incompetence, have admitted their failure, and have abdicated," Roosevelt said in the tones of William Jennings Bryan. ". . . The money changers have fled from their high seats in the Temple of our civilization. We may now restore that temple to the ancient truths."

The federal government, especially the President, had to put things right: "This Nation asks for action, and action now. Our greatest primary task is to put people to work . . . I shall ask the Congress for the remaining instrument to meet the crisis—broad Executive power to wage a war against the emergency, as great as the power that would be given to me if we were in fact invaded by a foreign foe. . . ."

As great as the power that Wilson had exercised during the previous war, and as great as the power in which Theodore Roosevelt had believed; the earlier Roosevelt, his distant cousin and his wife's uncle, had been, so Franklin Roosevelt sometimes said, the greatest man he had ever known. Wilson, whom the younger Roosevelt also admired, had appointed him assistant secretary of the navy, his first federal office, from which he had participated in the councils first of national reform and then of national mobilization. Like his illustrious progressive predecessors, Franklin Roosevelt was unafraid of power and responsibility. Or of life: felled in 1921 by poliomyelitis which deprived him permanently of the use of his legs, he had otherwise conquered the disease, learned to walk on braces and with canes, and returned to politics with a manner so outgoing and debonair that it ordinarily hid the toughness of his spirit and the determination of his ambition. "First of all," he said at the outset of his inaugural, "let me assert my firm belief that the only thing we have to fear is fear itself—nameless, unreasoning, unjustified terror."

Roosevelt's élan refreshed the hopes of his countrymen, even those who had twisted the rules of exchange. The Congress, also stirred, granted him emergency powers and rushed through his first proposals without hesitation or debate. Contrived to stop panic, those measures and others that soon supplemented them revealed the President's enduring purpose—not to abandon capitalism but to protect the system by strengthening its institutions and guarding it against the follies of those who had for so long dominated it.

American bankers should have hailed Roosevelt as a savior. In the blackest hour they had ever known, the legislation he sponsored saved them from permanent collapse and reduced the risks on which they made their profits. The devastating contraction of values, of real estate and commercial assets alike, and the resulting illiquidity of the loans that banks had made, had left the banks, especially since 1930, without sufficient cash resources to meet the demands of their increasingly anxious depositors. As those anxieties rose, more and more runs by depositors forced even sound, though illiquid, banks to close. Panic fed panic until, just before the inauguration, many state governments had closed banks within their jurisdictions. Roosevelt immediately declared a "bank holiday" to give his advisers time to work out a scheme for an orderly resumption of business. He had no interest in nationalizing the banks, a course some bankers recommended. As he knew, if the federal government took over the banks, he could turn only to the bankers to run them. Instead he quickly sent to Congress the Emergency Banking Act of 1933, which passed on March 9. That measure permitted liquid banks within the Federal Reserve System to reopen under license from the Treasury Department, as most banks did. In order to make them liquid, the act enlarged the kinds of paper they could hold as reserves. It also provided for the appointment of federal "conservators," an encouraging new name for receivers, to assist banks still closed in returning to a healthy state.

The act stopped the panic but did not solve the problems that had provoked it. To that latter end, the President fostered other legislation that at once buttressed the banking system and protected the savings and properties of the middle class. The Federal Deposit Insurance Corporation, established by the Banking Act of June 1933, guaranteed individual bank deposits up to $5000, a figure that has since continually increased. For the vast majority of Americans, that guarantee eliminated the fears that had provoked runs on banks and thus assured banks that deposits would remain at a level permitting them to engage in their normal business activities, though the act also curtailed speculation on credit, one major practice that had brought on the crash in 1929. On the same day Congress passed the Farm Credit Act, a bill which encouraged the refinancing of farm mortgages on long terms and at low interest rates. Essential as a measure to help farmers retain ownership of their land, it was no less important for the banks which sold illiquid mortgages they held to the Farm Credit Administration. Similarly the Home Owners Loan Corporation, created three days earlier, refinanced the illiquid mortgages, particularly of middle-class householders, and thereby further increased the liquid assets of the banks. The new laws saved from foreclosure the farms and homes of millions of Americans, eased their monthly mortgage payments, and made the banks the ancillary beneficiaries of a sensible federal largess. Yet as the program of the New Deal developed, bankers by and large accepted their salvation as their due and rewarded Roosevelt with a surly animosity.

For his part, since the time of his inauguration he had been addressing more fundamental problems that he and his advisers had been considering for months. Most exigent was the need for federal funds for the impoverished unemployed, millions of men and women and their families who lacked the means to purchase food or shelter. Other millions—blue collar and clerical workers, proprietors of small enterprises, pharmacists, engineers—while still employed had exhausted their savings and lived on shriveled incomes. The lasting remedy for those misfortunes depended on the recovery of the economy·which in 1933 was operating at less than half of its capacity. Yet recovery unaccompanied by social and economic reform would restore the inequities of wealth and influence that Roosevelt was committed to correct.

Progressivism, the liberalism of Roosevelt's youth, spoke to social welfare but not to business cycles. The New Deal had to cope simultaneously with both. There existed in 1933 no body of economic doctrine adequate to guide federal policy in the achievement of recovery. There persisted then the earlier, often competing biases of agents of reform, some concerned primarily with power, structure, and efficiency, some with distributive social justice. The President, stimulated always by the clash of ideas, had counselors who put forward conflicting arguments about the proper priorities for his administration. The ultimate arbiter of policy, he followed now one, now another track, often several at once. Ready to experiment as long as necessary, he refused to let his hands be tied. He operated, he often said, on a twenty-four hour basis. But his was an eclectic, not ordinarily an indecisive mind. From the first he held to certain principles, all of which, so he judged, the voters honored in their thumping majorities for him. He hewed to the tradition of gradual reform. Distrustful of big business and finance, he was eager to win their cooperation but resolved to curtail their influence in American life, and to eliminate the abuses produced by that influence. He was no less committed to mitigating the wretchedness of the poor and the helpless. He believed the federal government to be the only authority capable of undertaking those tasks or of fostering recovery, and he considered the president the principal energizer of the government.

Those beliefs had not prevailed since Wilson's prime. Between 1920 and 1933, three Republican presidents had abandoned the agenda of progressivism, had staffed federal agencies with the representatives of the interests they were supposed to oversee, and had invited the continual erosion of the redistributive wartime revenue legislation. They had resisted the use of federal authority, for one example in the regulation of the distribution of hydroelectric power, for another in the initiation of antitrust prosecutions, for a third in the delivery of relief to the needy unemployed. Two of them—Warren G. Harding and Calvin Coolidge—had ordinarily deferred to the preferences of the Congress; all of them had been comfortable with conventional jurisprudence; one of them—Herbert C. Hoover, Roosevelt's immediate predecessor—had moved to mitigate some of the impact of depression largely under the prodding of Democrats and progressive Republicans on the Hill. By 1933 the presidency had lost the stature that Theodore Roosevelt and Wilson had given it, and the momentum of reform, so largely spent in 1917 before the mission of reform was satisfied, had vanished. To satisfy his principles, to advance his purpose, Franklin Roosevelt had to reverse a dozen years of entropy in Washington. He welcomed the chance.

With an urbanity devoid of progressive moralism, Roosevelt enjoyed politics and power. He savored the presidency. He relished the endless adventure of governing men. His panache obscured, except for his intimates, his recurrent seasons of uncertainty or hesitation. His personal qualities most became him when he settled upon a policy in which he had thoughtful confidence. So it was during the creative early months of his first administration. The recovery measures he then proposed also advanced reform, while other programs began the necessary provision of relief. For a time, the President and his advisers, pressed to act rapidly on many fronts, circumvented the question of priorities by starting bravely to attempt to do everything at once.

The rationalizers, the exponents of order and management, dominated the President's councils at that juncture. Less than two weeks after assuming office, he took their plan for agriculture to Congress, and in the spring he followed with their plan for industry. Congress quickly passed legislation incorporating both. "Agricultural adjustment," the New Deal's innovative scheme, proposed to raise prices of staple crops by reducing production, and to reduce production by paying farmers benefits for withdrawing acreage from planting or grazing according to a national plan. Though the adoption of such a plan required the vote in a referendum of a majority of affected farmers, the certainty of benefits payments and the prospect of higher prices guaranteed that majority. As the Agricultural Adjustment Administration, which ran the program, went about its work, prices did rise, though not steadily at first, and not necessarily because of the government's planning. The drought and infestations of plant diseases during the middle 1930's hurt the production of both food and fiber crops, perhaps more severely than did federal acreage allotments.

Benefit payments, based upon acreage withdrawn from use, flowed primarily to large landowners, some of them the lords of agribusiness. Indeed their representatives in Congress and in the lobbies besieging it exercised a large influence in the staffing and administration of the program. Their objective, a continuing federal subsidy for commercial agriculture, clashed with the interests of subsistence and tenant farmers, and of consumers. Ineligible for benefits, tenants and sharecroppers, especially in the cotton South, found themselves driven from the land that owners removed from cultivation. In an effort to help the unfortunate, a small group of lawyers within the Department of Agriculture lost their battle and their jobs. Only in 1937, with the establishment of the Farm Security Administration, did impoverished tenants and migrants begin to receive effective federal assistance.

Roosevelt's secretary of agriculture, Henry A. Wallace, who had been slow to recognize their plight, had from the beginning accepted the policy of deliberate scarcity only as a temporary necessity, a way in which agriculture could organize itself and administer crop prices in order to balance the power of organized industry. A dedicated planner himself, Wallace after 1937 redirected the programs of the AAA to stress land conservation and long-range market stability. His "ever normal granary" contemplated federal purchase and storage of surpluses in years of high production, and federal sales from the resulting accumulations in lean years, a system that would keep supplies and prices at levels satisfactory to growers and consumers alike. The onset of World War II and the accompanying leap in demand for American food crops prevented a proper test of that plan, and opened the way for the farm lobby to extract swollen subsidies from a responsive Congress. The rationalization of agriculture, as it worked out, achieved a recovery of prices and farm incomes only with the fortuitous assistance of an angry nature, delayed federal aid for the distressed majority of rural Americans, and left an expensive legacy of special privileges for the big business of commercial farming.

The President had not planned it that way, any more than he planned the consequences of the program for rationalizing industry. Authorized by the National Recovery Act of 1933, that program carried Roosevelt's enthusiastic hopes for the achievement of the statute's title. It brought together several different expectations about national economic planning. One group of rationalizers, devoted social reformers like Rexford G. Tugwell, the handsomest of Roosevelt's "brains trust," believed that an orderly management of industrial affairs under government direction could result both in greater production and more general and equitable distribution of the wealth produced. Organized labor looked forward to playing a role in national industrial planning in order to stimulate the union movement. Rationalizers among businessmen, convinced as usual of the destructiveness of competition and the desirability of coordinating production to sustain prices and profits, anticipated that the federal government would delegate its planning authority to representatives of business interests, as it had, by and large, during World War I. The enabling legislation left open all those possibilities. It suspended the antitrust laws. It provided apparent guarantees of the right of labor to organize and bargain collectively. It gave the president the power through the promulgation of codes of fair competition "to promote the organization of industry for the purpose of cooperative action among trade groups."

To implement the act, Roosevelt established the National Recovery Administration under the direction of General Hugh S. Johnson, a veteran of Woodrow Wilson's War Industries Board. Colorful in manner and pungent in speech, Johnson chose to use wartime techniques of propaganda and public relations to promote voluntary adherence to the codes which he and his staff started to negotiate. In order to speed that process, he also prepared a blanket code setting standards for minimum wages and maximum hours. He also organized rallies and parades to publicize the NRA and to give luster to its symbol of compliance, a blue eagle. That hoopla and their own eagerness for any antidote to depression brought two million employers to sign the blanket code. The regular codes proved harder to arrange. The NRA relied on representatives of industry, labor, and consumers to work them out, but it proved difficult to determine who represented consumers or just what consumer interests were; and the independent unions had little experience with the major national industries, most of which they had never been able to organize. Consequently industrial representatives guided the making of codes, especially the provisions for controlling production and sustaining prices. Even so, some manufacturers refused to comply, often because of the concessions labor received. For his part, Johnson, too often engrossed by the problems of small and local industries, declined to use his coercive authority for fear of provoking a judicial test of the constitutionality of the NRA.

By the time Roosevelt forced Johnson out in 1934, enthusiasm for the NRA had disappeared. The price-fixing in the codes confirmed the fears of the original opponents of the program that it would foster monopoly. The complexity of many codes demonstrated that planning could become a clumsy as well as threatening substitute for competition. More important, industry-wide agreements limiting production and fixing prices artificially protected marginal firms operating with obsolete and inefficient equipment. Without the lure of a larger share of market and consequent increases in profits, more efficient enterprisers hesitated to expand production or invest in new machinery. Since recovery depended on new investments the NRA was inadvertently blocking its major purpose.

Before the Supreme Court declared the National Recovery Act unconstitutional in 1935, the NRA had nevertheless succeeded in furthering long-deferred social reforms. The codes established the principle of federal determination of minimum wages and maximum hours, a principle preserved by the Fair Labor Standards Act of 1938. The codes also effectively abolished child labor, an humane objective previously deferred first by the courts and then by southern resistance to a constitutional amendment. The boost that NRA gave to the unions animated the resurgence of the labor movement. Recruiters told workers that the President wanted them to join unions; labor leaders began to organize the major industries, steel and automobiles included, on an industry-wide basis that substituted vertical for crafts unions and thereby brought the unskilled into the movement. In spite of the resistance of management and the hostility of Hugh Johnson and other NRA officers, the most ebullient era of American labor history got underway.

With the demise of NRA, Roosevelt came to support the pending Wagner bill, earlier introduced by Robert Wagner, a tough-minded social reformer, accomplished politician, and Democratic senator from New York. A landmark statute passed in 1935, the act encouraged the organization of industrial unions and created the National Labor Relations Board to resolve disputes between labor and management. Under the government's friendly supervision, big labor emerged by 1941 as a powerful force in American industrial life, within the Democratic party, and in the lobbies on the Hill. Yet from 1933 onward, the renaissance of the labor movement, an essential engine of industrial justice, met the fierce antagonism of business managers whose resistance to unionization clashed with labor's new militancy. The accompanying violence during many of the resulting strikes, though provoked largely by the intransigence of management, persuaded the more conventional among the middle class that labor had become radicalized. Some unions did suffer from the infiltration of communists or gangsters, and the conflict between the two major labor organizations—the American Federation of Labor and the Congress of Industrial Organizations—in itself aggravated labor unrest, but the large majority of labor leaders were pursuing legitimate and legal ends that the New Deal endorsed. Their growing success nevertheless frightened the wealthy, both within and without management groups, and in some degree dampened their willingness to invest. If there was not a contradiction, there was at least a tension between the demands of reform and the needs of recovery. Roosevelt's bold initiatives notwithstanding, his New Deal could not do everything at once.

The President in any case had never counted exclusively on the rationalizers to provide direction for recovery or reform. The metaphor of the money changers in his inaugural address signaled his distrust not of bankers only but also of conventional monetary policy. Attentive during his campaign to advocates of inflation, he brought to the White House an abiding suspicion of Wall Street and its counsels. Though the banking legislation of 1933 did not threaten the financial community, Roosevelt began in April to take a series of steps calculated to inflate artificially the dollar, to transport the center of financial power from New York to Washington, and to insure continuing low interest rates, "easy money." Inflation in itself would ease the burden of debt, including the federal debt, existing or potential, and easy money would invite, though it could not guarantee, new private investment.

By 1933 the American dollar had suffered from several years of sharp deflation. As prices fell during the Depression, the real value of the dollar rose. A controlled inflation, "reflation" in the phrase of the time, would serve as a corrective, as Roosevelt saw it, on several counts. It would relieve agricultural debtors whose mortgages had become onerous with the deflation of commodity prices and land values. It would restore the balance between deeply depressed commodity prices and industrial prices which industry had been able to sustain by reducing production to the level of diminishing demand, a practice that Thorstein Veblen, the extraordinary American economic and social theorist, had earlier defined perceptively as sabotage. Further, Roosevelt considered the devaluation of the British pound in 1931 a deliberate act to cheapen sterling in order to gain larger markets for British exporters. A comparable devaluation of the dollar would erase that advantage.

To those ends, Roosevelt intended to reverse the process that brought about deflation. With the collapse of the American economy after 1929, and the ensuing depression throughout the Western world, Europeans had begun to withdraw investments from the United States. They did so by selling their properties for dollars, converting their dollars to gold, and repatriating that gold. As the standard for the dollar and most other major currencies, gold provided a primary basis for issuing currency and credits. As American gold flowed abroad, money and credit contracted, deflating the dollar. Though the banking legislation of March 1933 enlarged the basis for currency and credit, only a much greater expansion would permit the degree of reflation the President held desirable. That expansion mandated a departure from the gold standard, an end to free convertibility between gold and the dollar, an end to unsupervised gold flows between nations, as well as an end to the fixed ratio between the dollar and gold by weight.

An anathema to most of the banking and business community, the President's opinions about monetary policy had impressive support among Democrats in Congress. Indeed most of them were prepared to force him to inflation if he did not move that way himself. He had to use his large influence on the Hill to prevent the Senate from making mandatory an amendment to the agricultural act that gave him explicit permission to use several devices to inflate the currency. Farmers and their representatives who particularly pressed for inflation had substantial assistance from other groups, from monetary nuts, from special friends of silver and its monetization, and also from a nucleus of responsible economists and business leaders. That last cadre, which included the officers of J. P. Morgan and Company, had concluded that the gold standard was too constrictive to tolerate any longer. Various academic economists, of whom the most prestigious was Irving Fisher of Yale, believed that the federal government, once liberated from the artificial gold standard, should manage money values in the national interest, just as it could set import duties or regulate railroad rates.

Roosevelt's ventures in recovery through inflation proceeded from foundations in politics and analysis as broad and sound as those underlying rationalization, but he yielded on occasion to a glittering panacea that paraded as monetary theory. He began cautiously in April 1933 with an executive order that nationalized gold and made its exports subject to licensing by the Treasury. That order took the country off the gold standard without altering the fixed gold value of the dollar. During the summer the President cleared his path for more aggressive action. At the London Economic Conference, then meeting, the British hoped to tie all currencies to existing gold values which were favorable to their devalued pound; the French preferred to keep gold as the standard of international exchange. Under instructions from Roosevelt, the president's personal emissary opposed those objectives but agreed to a joint statement looking forward to a revised standard for exchange based upon gold. The President then rejected even that proposal in a brusque message that killed the conference. Though his tone was needlessly sharp, he protected his intention to keep his options open. He offended London and Paris but placated congressional inflationists who were increasingly agitated by a renewed decline in agricultural prices, which also worried him.

Perhaps the most simplistic of the monetary schemes then current addressed the problem by asserting a direct correlation between the price of gold and the price of other commodities. Beguiled by that proposition and its apparent vogue on the Hill, Roosevelt embarked in the autumn of 1933 on a temporary spree of gold buying. American purchases gradually raised the price of the metal to about $35 per ounce, a level at which the dollar, evaluated in terms of gold, had undergone about a 40 percent devaluation. The exercise shocked the traditionalists, among them many prominent Democrats and most financiers, some of whom predicted the imminent end of Western civilization, but the rising price of gold, contrary to the predictions of the panacea, did not lift commodity prices.

His experiment a failure, Roosevelt terminated it. Gold purchases continued, but at a steady $35 per ounce which the President asked Congress to establish, as it did in the Gold Act of 1934. On monetary matters he had acted to that time without explicit congressional approval. The statute granted that approval retroactively. It also provided him with authority he never used to alter further the price of gold. More important, it permitted the creation, as he had recommended, of a stabilization fund within the Treasury. That fund, based on the seigniorage the government gained from the increased dollar price of the gold it had nationalized, could buy and sell gold, dollars and other currencies in order, in Roosevelt's words, "to bring some greater degree of stability to foreign exchange rates." He had particularly in mind the use of the fund to protect the dollar from competitive manipulation of the pound. The fund could also buy and sell federal securities. That power permitted the Treasury, whatever the preferences of the Federal Reserve or the pressures of the money market, to keep government bonds, notes and bills at a constant value and thereby to establish and maintain low interest rates.

During the years of depression and war, the Treasury, by threatening to use its power, forced the Federal Reserve to pursue a cheap money policy. The Federal Reserve Board was a public agency, but an agency independent of and not accountable to the president. The Treasury, in contrast, was a political department, its secretary subject to the president's appointment or removal. With the Gold Act of 1934, the Treasury, Roosevelt's own arm, gained control over monetary policy for the duration of his administration. Political Washington eclipsed financial New York. And cheap money prevailed. It probably would have anyway, for until 1940 the lack of demand for commercial and industrial loans in itself kept interest rates down, while the growing flow of gold from a frightened Europe to a haven in the United States increased the American money supply and thus the availability of credit. But the Gold Act accomplished a major change in the balance of financial power within the United States. a change that infuriated most of Wall Street. The younger J. P. Morgan, who in 1933 applauded the departure from the gold standard, so detested the President by 1934 that he forbade the mention of Roosevelt's name in his presence.

Wall Street suffered another loss of power to the government in the Banking Act of 1935. The legislation of 1933 had left unaltered the basic structure of the Federal Reserve System. In 1934 Roosevelt turned to Marriner Eccles to design significant changes in that structure. An accomplished banker from Utah, Eccles brought his incisive but unconventional views to the drafting of the administration's bill. It met prolonged resistance from conservatives in both parties, but even in amended form it made fundamental revisions in the banking system. The act increased the range of authority of the Federal Reserve Board and reduced the independence of the regional Federal Reserve banks. The New York bank at last became subservient to the board in Washington. Eccles, whom Roosevelt appointed head of the latter body, fought off both the political influences of the Treasury and the traditional, professional influence of the New York bankers. Ultimately he succeeded in restoring the autonomy of the board, a public but not political agency, and in making it the major voice in national monetary policy. So long as he and Roosevelt remained in office, the board provided the quality of public service that the progressives had expected, as later did the New Dealers, from an expert federal agency.

Yet New Deal monetary policy and banking reform did not produce recovery. Low interest rates created a condition favorable to borrowing but could not in themselves excite investment. Regardless of the price of money, private investors remained unwilling to take risks in enterprises for which they saw no profitable future. They often blamed the New Deal, its gold buying or labor or other policies, for destroying their confidence, though they had displayed no confidence during the administration of their supposed champion, Herbert Hoover. For its part, the federal government, concerned legitimately about social and economic reform, failed to take advantage of the low interest rates it imposed. It did not itself borrow heavily enough for expenditures on public enterprises. In the event, monetary policy left its major imprint not on the depression or recovery but on enduring institutional reform.

Like his contemporaries, Roosevelt in 1933 had no understanding of the concept of deliberate, countercyclical, public spending to which J. M. Keynes, the great British economist, gave classic expression two years later. Clues to that road to recovery lay in Keynes' earlier work and that of other economists, but the President, his advisers and the Congress remained wedded, as did most businessmen and economists, to older and inhibiting doctrines, especially to a faith in the indispensability of a balanced federal budget. Though Roosevelt recommended and Congress approved unprecedented deficits, they accepted them not as a purposeful means to stimulate the economy but as a temporary and regrettable expedient. Early New Deal spending had two major objectives: to provide funds to assist the indigent unemployed, and to finance public work projects that would "prime the pump"—put enough charge into the economy to start it to function automatically again, as it allegedly had before 1929. Neither objective was adequate for recovery; both had significant social consequences.

As he had promised, Roosevelt made relief a top priority of his administration. With the Emergency Relief Act of 1933, the federal government for the first time in history recognized and assumed responsibility to assist directly the victims of depression. The act appropriated funds for dispersement to the states which then distributed the money to the needy unemployed. Harry Hopkins, whom the President appointed to take charge of the program, bent to his urgent task with refreshing speed. A former social worker whom Roosevelt had first recruited to public service in New York, Hopkins had a practical zeal for experimentation, and a personal style and charm that made him the most striking and useful of the New Dealers, an intimate of the President's, and a favorite target of partisan attack.

Dissatisfied with the dole, Hopkins developed a system of work relief which Congress authorized in a number of acts, the most important in 1935. Its terms allowed him to set up the Works Progress Administration and various subsidiary agencies. The WPA hired the unemployed to work directly on a variety of public projects, among them schools, parks, airports, post offices, and roads. Other projects Hopkins and his aides sponsored provided federal jobs for unemployed authors, actors, painters, musicians, school-teachers, lawyers, and engineers. One WPA subsidiary made grants to colleges to finance part-time employment for needy students. Though some of the early projects entailed little more than digging ditches or raking leaves, though no major project in the arts escaped the costs of personal and ideological rivalries among the participants, Hopkins succeeded in using relief not just to feed the unemployed but to renew their sense of self-esteem and of the dignity of work, and to nourish and preserve professional skills essential for American society and culture. That accomplishment gave a vital human cast to the government's innovative undertaking.

Hopkins' grand efforts did not much affect recovery. Neither the President nor the Congress, anxious about the federal budget, ever approved enough funds for work relief to reach all the unemployed who deserved it. Most Republicans and some Democrats considered the volume of expenditures dangerous and forms of relief other than the dole wasteful. Roosevelt was humane but prudent, his conservative critics, timid and penurious. From 1933 through 1940 appropriations for relief remained too small to quicken the economy. That outcome from the first required more money than even a broader work relief program could have spent.

Large scale public works offered the surest means for useful federal expenditures of a magnitude sufficient for recovery. The nation needed new highways, modern urban housing, great dams to control flooding and generate hydroelectric power—all of them beyond the reach and vision of private enterprise. Roosevelt understood those and even larger needs. His commitment accounted for the fulfillment of the dramatic dream, the complete rehabilitation of an entire region, through the Tennessee Valley Authority, which Congress established in 1933. He also envisaged a national system of superhighways, constructed long after his death. He realized, too, that federal public works would help the depressed construction industry, provide handsome orders for steel and concrete and building machinery, and thereby create new jobs for those who had been laid off. Accordingly he requested and Congress granted three billion dollars for public works as a part of the National Recovery Act. It was not yet clear that the sum, which seemed enormous to the men who calculated it, was an inadequate stimulus, or that the process of spending it would prove naggingly slow.

The public works program, Roosevelt's chosen means "to prime the pump," faltered partly because few plans existed in 1933 for appropriate federal projects. It took a long time to prepare designs for a dam, a bridge or a highway, and to acquire the land on which to build them. Harold Ickes, whom the President selected to oversee the program, had a characteristically progressive antipathy for waste or graft, and a conservationist's zeal for the beautification of the public domain. Those qualities subjected the planning of public works to meticulous but time-consuming review. As one observer remarked, Ickes spent money through a medicine dropper. The economy needed a cascade. Later in the decade, when Ickes had begun to move faster, private real estate interests blocked government efforts to build low-cost public housing. Further, though the New Deal nevertheless spent billions on public works, all of them of national value, neither the President nor the Congress, before the war in Europe began, even contemplated spending the hundred billions or more that would have created a deficit large enough to overcome the depression. They were beholden to fiscal prudence. Peacetime spending failed as a countercylical remedy because it was never tried.

The moneys that were spent would have had a more telling impact if the New Deal's revenue policy had not counteracted their potential effect. Roosevelt sponsored a series of tax proposals intended to generate more income for the government and designed also to promote economic reform, particularly to place the weight of taxation on Americans who could best afford to carry it. If the New Deal had reduced taxes, the resulting deficit would have exceeded those that materialized, possibly by enough to spur the economy. In that event, the United States might have experienced recovery without the reforms the President was seeking. But Roosevelt never intended merely to restore the conditions of the 1920's. The distribution of income and wealth during that decade struck most New Dealers as both unjust and unhealthy, unjust because the poorest third of the American people lived below a reasonable standard of comfort, unhealthy because that third and even the next third above them lacked the earnings and credit to sustain a level of consumption necessary for prosperity. Though that underconsumptionist theory had only partial validity, the New Dealers' moral outrage about the depth and range of poverty in the country had a sure foundation in democratic doctrine. Consequently Roosevelt was eager to make federal revenue policy an instrument for a broad redistribution of wealth and income.

Several of the more conservative among the President's advisers broke with him over the revenue bill he had the Treasury take to Congress in 1935, and conservative Democrats on the Hill weakened that measure. Still, the act as passed accomplished much of the Treasury's purpose, particularly by raising rates on middle and high incomes and large estates, and by graduating those rates more steeply. It was the most progressive revenue measure enacted in peacetime to that date. Because the Depression persisted, yields from the 1935 act did not reach their full dimension until the return of full employment in 1941. Only then and during the war years did the new schedules, and others added later, have the redistributive effect their supporters had intended.

The ultimate social gain had a large economic cost between 1935 and 1941, for in that period the impact of New Deal taxes braked recovery. The damage arose primarily from the level of the rates themselves and only marginally, if at all, from the adverse reaction of investors to the administration's frank decision to "soak the rich." The rich could afford it. Though the New Deal had saved their investments, they turned against Roosevelt before 1935. As the President put it the next year, with the normal exaggeration of a political campaigner, "they are unanimous in their hatred of me—and I welcome their hatred." The developing revenue program of the New Deal made that point as emphatically as did the President's rhetoric. Indeed many of the wealthy received a public flagellation in 1937 when the Treasury, with the President's encouragement, exposed the ways in which they had been dodging income taxes. The loopholes they had exploited were legal, though many of the techniques they used were devious. Congress closed most of the avenues of escape but, as before, the lawyers serving those seeking new ones soon found them.

The Revenue Act of 1935 had also attempted to strike at corporate size by taxing intercorporate dividends. That effort marked an early turning of the New Deal toward antitrust. Though corporate reorganization made the tax ineffectual, the Treasury tried again in 1936. Faced with a pending deficit, it recommended a novel and controversial tax on undistributed corporate earnings. In part the Treasury intended to force the distribution of profits by family-held corporations like the Ford Motor Company, for so long as profits were retained, the members of the family received little taxable income but the value of the stock they owned rose. More important, the advocates of the new tax believed that many large corporations were retaining much of their profits but not investing it. A tax that forced them to distribute all but a safe margin of profits would either provoke them to more investment or move cumulated profits to shareholders. Those profits, subject to the income tax, would also provide cash for alternative investment or consumer spending, both of which the economy needed.

Initially, with Roosevelt's approval, the Treasury proposed a graduated tax on undistributed earnings that exempted necessary reserves, gave special treatment to small corporations, and replaced all other existing taxes on corporations. Predictably that scheme excited the wrath of management. As the President and his counselors knew, capitalists, the owners of corporate stock, had not controlled major American corporations for many years. With rare exceptions, ownership was too widely dispersed to allow any investor a real voice in the policies of the companies on which he was betting. Professional managers exercised that control and meant to preserve their domain against any attack. Their lobbyists swarmed upon Congress. Conservative Democrats accepted the predictions of disaster with which those management spokesmen greeted the tax. Recalculations of its potential yield worried the budget-balancers. So persuaded, the Treasury retreated, as did the President. The Revenue Act of 1936 levied only a modified undistributed profits tax, against which the business community continued to lobby until its repeal in 1938. In the interval, in the opinion of economists friendly to business, the tax slowed investment. That judgment, if it was correct, constituted a self-fulfilling prophecy. Nevertheless the episode did again suggest that tax reform, in this instance a reform contrived to return capitalism to the capitalists, collided with recovery.

The prevailing obsession with the budget proved still more

debilitating in the cost of the social security program which Congress initiated, on the President's urging, in 1935. A long-deferred and vital social reform, it had emerged from the deliberations of a special committee Roosevelt appointed in 1933 to consider federal unemployment and old age insurance. At the insistence of the Treasury, the financing of the program rested on contributions from both employers and employees. Congress would have rejected any less prudential arrangement. Yet the payroll taxes on employees took income away from workers who needed it and reduced their purchasing power when the economy required it. Probably more than any other New Deal tax, the social security tax hurt recovery. Again, Roosevelt and the New Dealers could not accomplish everything at once.

They and the Congress could have achieved much more if they had had the economic sophistication and political courage to spend at a multiple of ten times or more the amount appropriated between 1933 and 1940. That measure of spending would have produced the desirable countercyclical results in spite of the yields from progressive taxation and the disenchantment of investors with other reforms. But the new economics came to Washington, indeed even to the academy, too late to inform policy. As late as 1939 the few advisers to Roosevelt who had embraced Keynesian doctrine had yet to convince the many who rejected it, and a heavy majority of the Congress remained opposed to deliberate deficit finance. As it worked out, both the prevailing myths about the budget and the friction between recovery and reform policies kept the public and private sectors alike from making the essential investments. Largely on that account the economy floundered in 1937, prices on the stock market dropped that autumn to disturbing lows, unemployment began to soar, and conditions in early 1938 returned to the grim levels of 1933. That recession brought Roosevelt for the first time to advocate counter-cyclical spending, though privately he hoped soon to return to conventional economics. The recession also contributed to

Democratic losses in November which left the control of Congress with a coalition of Republicans and conservative southern Democrats, a coalition that defeated the President's recovery program in 1939 and successfully opposed further reform during the rest of his time in office.

The paradoxical counterplay between recovery and reform had reflected the naïveté of Roosevelt's generation about economics and also raised the question of whether social progress could proceed vigorously in a time of depression. Had the President given sole priority to recovery, he would have risked creating a kind of fascist society. Had he made reform his only concern, he would have had to ignore the national condition and the expectations of the electorate. He had no choice but to pursue both goals simultaneously even in the absence of an economic doctrine that could have reconciled them. Keynesian formulations proved their worth during the war and provided the conceptual basis for the Employment Bill, passed in modified form in 1946, that Roosevelt in 1944 had begun to make central to his postwar program.

Like the progressives before him, Franklin Roosevelt intended from the beginning of the New Deal to save capitalism by reforming it. His liberalism, like theirs, had middle-class origins and goals. The New Deal moved far beyond the perimeters of earlier progressive striving. Agriculture, public utilities, the airlines and the truckers, the coal and oil industries, the banks and exchanges all felt the bite of federal authority. The success of the union movement and the enactment in peacetime of potentially redistributive revenue legislation gave the New Deal an egalitarian cast that most progressives would have resented. Yet the New Deal was radical if at all, in its scope, not in its purpose. Roosevelt reduced the risks upon which capitalism had often floundered and endeavored to enlarge the middle class and to ease access to it because those objectives infused his most enduring priorities. They explained the cryptic statement with which he described himself: "I am that kind of liberal because I am that kind of conservative."

Within the constraints imposed by the Depression, the New Deal encouraged long-standing American aspirations to own a farm or home, and to acquire a useful education and dignified employment. The economic bill of rights that Roosevelt pronounced in 1944 as part of his postwar program incorporated those aspirations. It included rights to a "useful and remunerative" job, to decent housing and to a good education, as well as to protection from the financial fears of old age, accident, sickness, and unemployment. The wartime GI bill delivered the substance of those rights to veterans, the only Americans to whom Congress was yet willing to extend Roosevelt's "new goals of happiness and well-being."

During both depression and war the President and his associates also recruited members of previously proscribed ethnic groups to elite positions in government and politics. Progressivism had attracted and relied upon a disproportionate number of white Protestant Americans, though by the early twentieth century and increasingly thereafter immigrants and second-generation Americans were gaining a growing voice within the Democratic party in the cities. To strengthen their allegiance the New Dealers unabashedly practiced recognition politics. Especially in the industrial states, the Democrats during the 1930's and 1940's ran balanced tickets characterized by the presence on them of Irish and Jewish candidates, often also of Italians or Poles. Without lowering previous standards of quality, Roosevelt also regularly drew from those and similar groups for appointment to the federal judiciary, to other major federal offices, and to the new agencies and informal councils of the New Deal. In so doing he reached into fresh reservoirs of talent and sensibility. Outsiders in American society understood their own problems better than did most old-stock observers. The President needed the ablest among those outsiders to devise and manage programs suitable to his purposes.

Eleanor Roosevelt pushed her husband to expand the recognition of women and blacks, long the victims of Washington's hostility or indifference. The Women's Bureau of the Democratic party drew women into politics. Roosevelt made Frances Perkins his secretary of labor, the first woman ever to join the cabinet. Within her domain and particularly also in Harry Hopkins', strong women, most of them alert to the special social problems of their sex, assumed responsible federal posts. Though their number seemed small by the standards of a later generation, Roosevelt went far beyond any of his predecessors in placing women in government. Blacks fared less well, partly because southern senators approved appointments only of their regional friends to federal offices in the southern states, including offices overseeing work relief which reached distressingly few southern blacks. Yet Roosevelt ended the lily-white practices of Republican administrations of the 1920's; New Dealers terminated the segregation of facilities within federal buildings in Washington, and at least a token coterie of black administrators reached influential positions. More important, in northern cities blacks received close to an equitable share of work relief and by 1936 most urban blacks, recipients also of favor from local Democratic leaders, had moved into the party of the New Deal. By 1940 blacks constituted a significant element within the Democratic coalition.

The New Deal did not complete the democratization of American political life; it did hasten that process. It did not remove prejudice from government; it did reduce it. Roosevelt neither started nor joined movements for equal rights for women or blacks. Those causes stood low in his order of priorities which put recovery and reform to the front until 1940, and victory above all else during the war. But Roosevelt and the New Deal gladly accepted the pluralism of American society and tempered the elitism of early century reformers by making the search for able governors continually inclusive instead of usually exclusive. The President attracted a constituency more varied than most progressives ever solicited and brought to the federal establishment, which he so happily expanded, a company of men and women from backgrounds as diverse as American society itself.

Among those who came to Washington were a sprinkling of the kind of outspoken radicals whom the earlier generation of reformers had scorned. The persisting Depression and rising menace of fascism during the 1930's gave to Marxism and to the Soviet Union a plausible though false allure. The Soviet Union seemed to the uncritical to have succeeded in planning an equitable society and to stand alone against fascist aggression. Those appearances, deceptive though they were, attracted thousands of Americans to Stalinism, to the Communist party, usually briefly, and usually innocently, to party-sponsored causes. A negligible number of men and women entered the underground service of the Soviet state. In the lower echelons of the federal government and among the beneficiaries of relief there were groups of radical dissenters, vocal and often conspiratorial, but proportionately little more numerous than their counterparts in cities across the country. Few party members gained important federal office; far fewer took any part in espionage; none significantly affected policy.

Though there was no Communist menace, a search for one provided a career of sorts for the head of the FBI and for some congressmen, natural vigilantes. Roosevelt joined none of their efforts. As he told one group of college students he had no use for Communism, but he also had no appetite for anti-Communism. He sought only assurance that Communists were not violating the laws. Though he never consciously invited radicals of any stripe to join his own councils, he was unafraid of radical dissent, permitted his associates to defend its expression, and expected the American people to reject its theories, as he had.

By expanding accessibility to federal office for Americans outside traditional elite groups, and by practicing a liberalism essentially devoid of traditional antiradicalism, Roosevelt largely escaped two of the several paradoxes that had characterized earlier reform presidents, but he did not escape them all. Like his predecessors, he retained an affection for rural values and country life, and he oscillated in his approaches to the problems of monopoly. His initial support for the programs of the rationalizers indicated an acceptance of bigness, oligopoly, and administered pricing as conditions of American society. Even after the failure and demise of the NRA, he continued to rely on regulatory agencies, which the New Deal created in new abundance, to oversee the activities of business and finance. By 1935 he had also begun to turn toward the antitrusters among his advisers. The Revenue Acts of 1935 and 1936 reflected their influences. So did the President's own increasingly antibusiness rhetoric, a style provoked in part by the patent hostility of business toward the New Deal.

With the coming of the recession in 1937, Roosevelt concluded that businessmen were withholding new investment in a kind of strike against him. He retaliated the next year by asking Congress for funds to investigate concentrations of economic power, a request that materialized in the creation of the Temporary National Economic Committee. Its voluminous reports described a degree of concentration in American industry that confirmed the assumptions of the antitrusters in Washington. Under the direction of one of them, Thurman Arnold, whom Roosevelt had appointed assistant attorney general, the Antitrust Division of the Justice Department had begun its most vigorous campaign in history. But that effort collapsed when the War and Navy Departments persuaded the President to suspend antitrust proceedings during the war. Though Arnold's successors carried a few of his most important cases to successful conclusion, federal wartime procurement policy helped to increase by two to three times the shares of market, income and resources of the largest American firms. Compared to the long-run implications of that development, Roosevelt's wavering intentions about antitrust policy had little enduring significance. Even the regulatory agencies, vigorous and innovative while the New Dealers staffed them, lapsed into torpidity and captivity soon after the war. On the question of monopoly, the legacy of the New Deal, like that of the progressives, remained as ambiguous as the President's attitude.

Roosevelt's conception and use of his office had an immediate and persisting impact. In the manner of Theodore Roosevelt and Woodrow Wilson, he interpreted his authority broadly, took and held center stage in public life, and employed his resulting influence with a grand style that at times concealed his intermittent caution in managing the political process. Journalists, delighted by his frequent and open press conferences, valued his frankness, not the least his off-the-record asides, enjoyed his humor and repartee, and as a group supported the New Deal with as much fervor as most of their editors opposed it. The radio, amplifier for his bully pulpit, provided him with a medium in which he excelled. His celebrated "fireside chats," couched in a homey eloquence, reached millions of Americans who came to feel they were his friends, as he told them they were.

Most of his subordinates developed an affection for him that held their loyalty even when they realized he was manipulating them. Manipulate them he did, now teasing, now joking, now speeding the departure of insistent guests by arranging for Falla—his Scottie—to lick his luncheon plate or wet the rug, by assigning regularly to several eager men a common problem in order to encourage each of them to compete to provide the best solution. He could then decide among their proposals; he alone retained the ultimate power. He even joked about that practice. "Bring it to Papa," Roosevelt told his political children when they wrangled over a complex issue. But he also held their hands when he had ruffled their egos or when their sibling rivalries led to public brawls. The hand-holding sufficiently overcame their occasional disappointments with him to keep most of them from succumbing to an ambivalent impulse to resign. As he knew, they did not really want to leave home; they needed only reassurances from Papa. Roosevelt's administrative style sometimes seemed sloppy or confused. In fact it was as calculated as it was personal, and by and large it worked.

So usually did his now calculated, now intuitive approach to politics. Even before 1932 he began to rebuild the coalition that had elected Wilson, and by 1936 he had expanded it to make the Democratic party the dominant party in the country for another generation. The program of the New Deal made that achievement possible; the politics of the White House made it certain. The President unabashedly cultivated the leaders of the party organization in the cities—Kelly and Nash in Chicago, Hague in Jersey City, Pendergast in Kansas City. In New York, where his relations with Tammany faltered, he helped to build up the power of Mayor Fiorello La Guardia who brought together liberal Democrats, independent Republicans, and organized labor. Roosevelt also nurtured friendships with senior southern Democrats and maverick midwestern progressives. By 1936 the labor vote, the urban vote, the solid South, the agricultural West, most blacks, and most middle-class intellectuals had joined beneath the Democratic banner. There they stayed in uncomfortable harness so long as Roosevelt ran for office.

By 1936 the President had also enlarged the staff and increased the versatility of the executive office. To it, as Wilson had during the war, he attached special agencies and also special assistants to help in drafting legislation and speeches, for liaison with Congress, and to undertake assignments that did not neatly fit the sphere or temper of any cabinet departments. The White House staff provided Roosevelt with an imperium of his own. In the increasingly complex circumstances of the nation and the world, he could not have governed without it, nor could he have managed the sweeping programs that Congress had enacted, programs which depended for implementation upon a large and strong federal executive. By 1936, Roosevelt had mastered his office and his party, won the electorate, and moved Congress and the federal establishment to unprecedented creativity. He was, as he said, the issue that year, and only Maine and Vermont fell away from his fold.

Yet in 1935 and 1936, years of marked success for Roosevelt, the Supreme Court handed down a series of decisions that called into question the President's authority to govern according to the policies of the New Deal. Those decisions reiterated judicial doctrines that had troubled progressives at the turn of the century. In the interval, the views of a majority of the court had remained fixed. Though the membership of the court had changed, it continued to block social and economic reform.

A first of the court's crippling decisions of 1935 declared the NRA unconstitutional. All nine justices agreed that the transfer of authority over the regulation of industry from the Congress to the President to the code makers was "delegation run riot." In a further ruling, the five conservatives held that the National Recovery Act went beyond the authority of Congress over interstate commerce. That contention earned Roosevelt's description of the decision as "horse and buggy" jurisprudence. Similarly constricted interpretations of the commerce power brought a majority of the court to invalidate New Deal legislation establishing a pension system for railroads, and minimum wages and maximum hours in the coal industry. The majority also knocked out state wages-and-hours legislation by recourse to their nineteenth-century tenet about due process. In 1936 the court also struck down the Agricultural Adjustment Act on the basis of a tortured and stultifying reading of Congress's power to tax.

Those decisions provoked hot criticism even from moderates in Congress and among journalists and other commentators. As they observed, the court was saying in effect that the federal government could do nothing for industry, labor, or agriculture to mitigate economic crisis. Critics of the decisions, including dissenters on the court itself, rehearsed the arguments against judicial infallibility and for judicial restraint. But the intransigent justices, all but McReynolds appointees of Republican presidents, had long since closed their minds to those arguments. If their opinions continued to prevail, the court would predictably invalidate the Wagner Act, the Social Security Act, and much of the rest of the New Deal's achievement. As Roosevelt told his cabinet, that outcome could lead to marching in the streets. He could see three possible preventives: a constitutional amendment declaring the uninhibited power of Congress over interstate commerce; an amendment restricting the authority of the court; or the appointment of new judges (as Lincoln and Grant had done) to create a majority sympathetic to the New Deal.

Though the last of those courses struck the President as a "distasteful possibility," it offered the quickest solution. The sweeping Democratic victory and his own smashing mandate in 1936 made it appear feasible. With the Republicans pushed back to the precincts and increased Democratic majorities on the Hill, Roosevelt moved to pack the court. To the Congress that convened in 1937, he sent a surprise message, drafted after private consultation with the attorney general, that called for the appointment of an extra justice for each sitting justice past the age of seventy. In support of that proposal Roosevelt held that the court was behind in its work. That disingenuous argument offended all the justices, the liberals included, and particularly the chief justice. It was also inaccurate, as the chief demonstrated, about the court's calendar. The Democratic leadership in Congress, stunned by the plan, had had no time to muster support for it. Any scheme to enlarge the court would have aroused opposition in Congress, but Roosevelt's proposal and his awkward tactics in making it gave the opposition an immediate advantage.

The President's bill failed. Worse, it split the Democrats in the Senate into two wrangling factions. Their long debate about the court, which the Republicans watched with delight, held up other important legislation, including the Fair Labor Standards bill and a second Agricultural Adjustment bill which did not pass until 1938. The emotions the court plan evoked, in Congress and out, and the common contention of conservatives that Roosevelt was trying to become a dictator, spilled over to delay approval for his sound recommendation for a major reorganization of the executive branch. The venture in court packing also complicated relations between the President and the Congress, and contributed, with the recession, to Democratic losses in the elections of 1938. After those losses, Republicans and southern Democrats in coalition could and did block further social reform, pare appropriations for domestic programs, and challenge the authority of New Deal regulatory agencies.

The Supreme Court escaped further attack largely because the successive retirements or deaths of the horse-and-buggy justices allowed Roosevelt to appoint successors for them who then overturned the rulings that had been made. Decisions rendered from 1937 through 1940 gave a latitudinarian definition to the commerce and taxing powers of Congress, and a procedural rather than a substantive definition to due process. In a sense Roosevelt had won the jurisprudential battle, but only at the cost of losing the momentum of the New Deal. Reform might have faltered in any event, for with the outbreak of war in Europe in 1939, the President had to give a high priority to questions of national defense and foreign policy, a priority detrimental to the domestic objectives which the most dedicated New Dealers still wanted to pursue.

Franklin Roosevelt approached foreign policy from the perspective of two mutually abrasive precedents. In large degree a disciple of Theodore Roosevelt, he understood the importance of political realism in foreign affairs and in preserving world order, and he believed in maintaining a strong navy, and later in building a strong air force, for American defence. Influenced also by Woodrow Wilson, he was restive with the imperialism of the first Roosevelt and of Western European powers, and he retained a sentimental attachment to the internationalism of the League of Nations as Wilson had envisaged it. In 1933 that sentiment lay submerged. Roosevelt accommodated to the national mood of the 1930's that rejected Wilsonian principles, even as that mood expressed itself in myopic isolationism from Europe. But the new President sounded a note of peace and self-restraint in his inaugural: "I would dedicate this Nation to the policy of the good neighbor—the neighbor who resolutely respects himself and, because he does so, respects the rights of others—the neighbor who respects his obligations and respects the sanctity of his agreements in and with a world of neighbors."

That commitment provided the foundation for policy in Latin America. In 1933 at the Pan-American Conference at Montevideo, the United States endorsed the proposal of its neighbors that "no state has the right to intervene in the internal or external affairs of another." Roosevelt held to that promise even in dealing with Mexico which expropriated the holdings of foreign-owned oil companies. Through the Export-Import Bank the administration also extended development loans to various Latin American governments. By 1939 hemispheric relations had become more amicable than ever before.

Roosevelt's first foreign economic policies had obvious nationalistic leanings. The rupture of the London Economic Conference in 1933 and the anti-British bias of the Gold Act of 1934 demonstrated that the President gave domestic considerations a priority over international cooperation on monetary matters. He also cultivated American exports while pursuing a liberalization of world trade through the reciprocity treaties which his secretary of state, Cordell Hull, considered vehicles for peace as well as prosperity.

Those developments carried little weight in the turbulent world of the 1930's. Roosevelt had no illusions about the growing crises in Europe and Asia. Just before he took office, Henry L. Stimson, the outgoing secretary of state, briefed him about the recent Japanese accession of Manchuria and the gloomy set of Japanese ambitions in China. The President also never doubted that the rise of Adolf Hitler to power in Germany in 1933 foreboded war in Europe. In that year both Germany and Japan withdrew from the League of Nations and began ominous armament programs. For his part, Roosevelt allocated some public work funds into naval building, neglected for over a decade. More important, he undertook negotiations that led to formal American recognition of the Soviet Union. Since 1917 the American policy of nonrecognition had offended the Soviet government without weakening it. By 1933 some American businessmen fancied they could find a new market in Russia. Roosevelt cared much more about bringing the Soviet Union into the balance against Germany in Europe and Japan in Asia. In moving as he did, he ignored the advice of the permanent officers of the State Department and the Foreign Service. He had no use for the "striped-pants crowd" or their conventional mentality. Especially did he disdain their unreflective anti-Communism. For a dozen years they had subscribed to a domino theory postulating that a Soviet gain in Latvia or Estonia would topple over a series of connected blocks, successively in Eastern, Central and Western Europe, until the whole continent had become permanently red. Partly because the Foreign Service persisted in its rigid ways, largely because the Soviet Union was at least equally inflexible, relations between the United States and Russia remained strained, but Roosevelt's recognition of the Soviet Union, which improved them, reflected the President's sensitivity for practical world politics.

He had little room in which to maneuver. Successive initiatives for disarmament stumbled against the intransigence of Hitler in Germany and Benito Mussolini in Italy. Great Britain and France, buried in depression, responded indecisively to Germany's resurgence. Divided and disorganized, China could not defend herself against the further encroachments which Japan began in 1937. The United States, as Roosevelt knew, had neither the means nor the will to police the world during the 1930s, nor in that decade were other democratic nations prepared to share that task. Indeed the President, like his countrymen and Congress especially, was unwilling even to consider a recourse to arms on any distant continent.

In 1934 the Senate even rejected Roosevelt's recommendation that the United States join the World Court. That small gesture toward internationalism, which many eminent Republicans favored, struck isolationists in both parties as corrupting of American sovereignty. The hearings they staged the following year confirmed their assumption that exports of arms to the Allies and Wilson's defense of neutral rights had needlessly drawn the country into war in 1917. The Senate then passed a neutrality bill forbidding those practices. The measure left the President with no latitude to discriminate between aggressors and victims of aggression, no flexibility of policy. He needed to use all his influence to secure enactment of a modified bill granting him discretionary authority, though even it kept mandatory the embargo on arms. Other legislation prohibited loans to nations in default to the United States, in effect to all the European powers. In 1937 Congress permitted the President to invoke the neutrality legislation by deciding whether a state of war existed, but not until after the outbreak of the war in Europe in 1939 did a further revision, for which Roosevelt had to struggle, permit belligerents to purchase arms in the United States and to carry them on their own ships to their destination. Under those conditions, there was little either of realism or of internationalism that Roosevelt could venture.

For his part, the President during the 1930s shared the national reluctance to become involved again in a war in Europe.

Nevertheless anxious about the growing strength of the fascist countries, he was inclined, as a man of principle, to stronger action that he could undertake as president. The conflict between his personal impulses and his sense of political possibilities resulted in periods of caution and irresolution that no one in his situation could have avoided. Until 1940 he could not and did not take any effective step against aggression that depended upon congressional or public consent.

Within the area of his own discretion, Roosevelt made some inconclusive gestures to deter the Germans and Japanese. Persuaded in 1936 that the new antifascist government of France needed American and British encouragement to survive and moved by French pleas, the President permitted the Treasury to negotiate the Tripartite Stabilization Agreement. A major modification of his policy at the London Conference in 1933, the pact established a system of consultation through which each of the signatories could adjust the value of its currency in consultation with the others and without fear of competitive devaluation. Though technical in nature, the agreement grew out of political motives. So also did Roosevelt's invocations of a section in the tariff laws that mandated retaliation against German and later Italian export subsidies. Roosevelt also declined to declare the existence of a state of war in China, which Japan had invaded. He thereby avoided the application of the neutrality laws which would have prevented the Chinese from obtaining even the trickle of supply they received from purchases in the United States. Twice the President considered stronger measures. In 1937, after Japanese airplanes sank the American gunboat *Panay* on the Yangtze River, he contemplated seizing Japanese assets in the United States. In 1938, during the crisis in Europe over Hitler's demands on Czechoslovakia, he studied ways in which to assist the British and French in financing the purchase of American arms. On both occasions he pulled back partly because the tactics in question seemed oblique to his purposes, but largely because he feared adverse public reactions to them. Then and later, as he liked to say, he could not afford to get out too far ahead of his army—of public opinion in general and congressional opinion in particular.

He did try to warn the country. "War is a contagion," he told the American people in 1937. ". . . It can engulf states and peoples remote from the original scene of hostilities. We are determined to keep out of war, yet we cannot insure ourselves against the disastrous affects of war and the dangers of involvement." When he made that speech he had in mind the use of economic sanctions against aggressors, but the explosive response to the address persuaded him to reject that course.

Instead he adopted a clandestine technique. After England and France capitulated to Hitler at Munich in 1938, Roosevelt arranged, over the objections of the War Department, to assist the French in negotiating to purchase some late-model American military aircraft. He was eager to facilitate their rearmament and equally to obtain their financing of additional American plants and machinery at a time when Congress would not appropriate funds for that purpose. The crash of a test plane carrying a French observer exposed that scheme which Senate critics condemned during hearings in 1939. The French and British were able to buy American planes only after the onset of war and the revision of neutrality legislation.

War came in a manner that surprised even those American observers who had understood Hitler's ambitions. Long antagonists, Germany and the Soviet Union signed a nonaggression pact in August 1939 that divided Poland between them. Germany then invaded Poland and on September 3, Great Britain and France, convinced of the futility of further appeasement, declared war on Germany. In a fireside address Roosevelt repeated his determination to keep war from the United States but pretended to no neutrality of thought. "Even a neutral," he said, "cannot be asked to close his mind or his conscience." Yet in the next months

Congress did almost that. During the winter of 1940 the war in the west barely simmered but the Soviet Union seized Latvia, Estonia, and Lithuania as well as the eastern third of Poland, and attacked Finland—aggressions undertaken in the name of defense. In spite of American sympathy for the Finns, who resisted gallantly, the President and State Department, sensitive to congressional sentiment, made only a cautious proposal for aid to Finland. Even that step evoked strong opposition from isolationists who feared setting any precedent that might result in assistance to England and France. The token aid finally offered became available only when the Finns were at the verge of defeat. They capitulated in March 1940. To that date Roosevelt was still captive of political conditions that contained his own personal impulses to move more vigorously in behalf of Germany's enemies, the remaining defenders of the eastern Atlantic.

Hitler's blitzkrieg in the spring of 1940 shocked the American public, until then still largely complacent about the potential impact of the European war. Between early April and late June, Denmark, Norway, the Netherlands, Belgium, and France fell to the Nazis, and British forces on the continent, their heavy equipment abandoned, barely escaped across the channel. With Great Britain standing alone, led now by Winston Churchill whose spirit and oratory stirred many Americans as much as they did his own people, public opinion moved rapidly, though not universally, toward support of aid to the British short of war. A majority in Congress, in contrast, while eager at last to vote appropriations for Roosevelt's national defense program, remained skittish about providing direct help to England. For the rest of the year the President had to operate on his own to that end.

Roosevelt resorted to the full powers of his office because he felt the urgency of Britain's plight and doubted Congress would authorize the extraordinary steps he took. Yet he made his purpose public. "We will pursue two obvious and simultaneous courses," he announced in June 1940. "We will extend to the opponents of force the material resources of this nation, and . . . we will harness and speed up the use of these resources in order that we ourselves . . . may have equipment equal to the task of any emergency and every defense." Responding to a plea from Churchill, he arranged for the sale of surplus rifles, cannon, ammunition, and other equipment left over from the first world war and now essential for the defense of England against a German invasion. The authority for that transaction rested upon a statute of 1919 governing the disposal of surplus, and on a loophole in the neutrality laws that permitted the sale of arms to American firms which could resell them for cash. In spite of England's needs, neither the law nor the state of national defense permitted the alienation of the newest and best American weapons such as the B-17 long-range bombers or the fast motor-torpedo boats of which there were far too few for the adequate supply of the air force and navy.

While husbanding those weapons, the President and his agents made the British pay for everything they did receive. To obtain the dollars to defray those costs, England had to liquidate most of her gold and sell much of the stock her citizens had owned in American corporations. Before the end of 1940 Britain had just about exhausted her financial resources. To meet her continuing, desperate needs, particularly for destroyers to protect the convoys carrying American equipment across the Atlantic, Roosevelt and Churchill worked out an ingenious agreement. Though neither principal would call it an exchange, it was so by any other name. The United States, on the basis of long-term leases, took over seven British bases in North America and the Caribbean, bases vital to American defense and beyond England's ability any longer to sustain. The British received fifty surplus American destroyers, critical for their war against German submarines but of no immediate use to the American navy.

The destroyer deal, executed during the presidential campaign of 1940, would have been politically impossible had not Roosevelt secured prior acceptance of it from the Republican candidate, Wendell Willkie. Roosevelt had earlier strengthened his administration and wooed Republicans who favored aid to England by appointing Henry L. Stimson secretary of war and Frank Knox secretary of the navy. Those eminent elders of the GOP participated in the discussions leading up to the destroyer exchange and supported the Conscription Act that Congress passed in 1940, the first peacetime draft in American history. They brought to their departments recruits from the high ranks of business, finance, and corporate law whose presence in Washingron, like their own, reassured habitual critics of the New Deal. The weight of Republican sympathy for aid to England accounted in large part for Willkie's surprise victory at the national convention which had been expected to nominate either Senator Robert A. Taft of Ohio or Governor Thomas E. Dewey of New York, both then isolationists. But the growing public enthusiasm for assisting England short of war did not overcome the powerful opposition to that policy of a vocal minority of Americans, some quarter or more of the electorate, and did not extend to any substantial support for entering the war. On that account Willkie in his campaign employed a rhetoric more insular than were his beliefs. For his part, Roosevelt in a celebrated speech in Boston began by proudly reviewing the record of what he had done for Great Britain and ended by promising never to send American boys to fight a foreign war.

Only by engaging in a fervent and evasive hope could the President, like most of his countrymen, reconcile that justified boast with the flimsy assurance. Robert Taft, perhaps the most intelligent as well as the most refractory of the President's opponents, warned that the provision of increasing aid to England would carry the United States into the battle itself. Privately some of Roosevelt's close advisers, among them Secretaries Stimson, Harold Ickes of the Interior Department, and Henry Morgenthau of the Treasury, had come to the same realization, which they strove to subdue. Unlike Taft, they considered the risk of war less dangerous to American interests than the risk of England's defeat and a Nazi triumph in Europe. Roosevelt seemed to sustain confidence in the concurrent pursuit of both parts of his policy. Following his re-election, he subjected that policy to a severe test on the Hill.

Churchill informed the President in December 1940 that Great Britain could no longer find the cash to pay for American weapons, nor could she survive without an assured supply of American-made warships, airplanes, tanks and other heavy military gear. Roosevelt had then to contrive some way of satisfying British requirements without recourse to forbidden loans; as he put it, he had "to get away from a dollar sign." He incorporated that objective in Lend-Lease bill of January 1941. Its terms empowered the President to sell, exchange, lend or lease war equipment and materials to the government of any nation "whose defense the President deems vital to the defense of the United States."

The bill immediately raised a storm. Leading isolationists condemned it as an irrevocable leap toward war. The majority of Republicans in Congress opposed it also as a surrender of authority to the President. But after two months of hearings and debate, most Democrats, including conservatives mollified by Roosevelt's retreat from reform, stood behind the measure, and their votes, along with those of Republican internationalists, carried the bill by safe margins. Still, it passed only after amendments stipulating that nothing in it should be construed to give the President the power to use the navy to convoy belligerent ships, and that the President was to report to Congress every ninety days about everything to do with lend-lease that he could divulge without injury to the public interest. Congress in its turn could monitor the act periodically before voting the appropriations necessary for its execution. Over the next four years the Senate kept a close watch on the volume of lend-lease expenditures, on the designation of recipients, and on the conditions it deemed relevant to national defense. Though the act increased Roosevelt's freedom of action and made the United States, as he said, "the arsenal of democracy," it bound him to continual congressional scrutiny.

The inception of lend-lease rapidly demonstrated that a commitment to supply Great Britain in order to defend America could not stop at the waterline. During the rest of 1941 German submarines destroyed British shipping twice as fast as it could be replaced. "The crunch of the whole war," in Churchill's words, lay on the Atlantic Ocean. Roosevelt, of the same mind, in April 1941 negotiated an agreement to dispatch American troops to Greenland, a Danish possession that lay within the Western Hemisphere, so long recognized as an area of special American concern. In May he proclaimed a state of "unlimited national emergency" which activated some ninety-nine statutes giving the president special powers. His proclamation referred specifically to the need "to repel any . . . acts or threats of aggression directed against any part of the Western Hemisphere." To that end, in July he made an executive agreement with Iceland, which lay beyond the hemisphere, to send American troops there. Had the Nazis seized Iceland, they would have threatened the Americas, as he said, and enhanced their ability to interrupt the flow of weapons to England, "a matter of broad policy approved by Congress." Denying the existence of any threat, Senator Taft protested that decision. Roosevelt, he argued, was nullifying the power of Congress to declare war. The constitutional authority of the president as commander in chief, however, as past precedents suggested, allowed Roosevelt to go at least as far as he had in the movement of armed forces to deter a threat he perceived.

Roosevelt needed no reminder that Congress had large powers of its own. During the summer of 1941, with England still in peril and the Nazis racing eastward after their invasion of the Soviet Union, the House of Representatives renewed the Conscription Act by a margin of only one vote. Believing as he did that the United States was in increasing danger, Roosevelt saw no alternative to proceeding still further in the Atlantic without the certain delays and possibility for defeat he would have risked by soliciting explicit congressional approval. On his own he ordered the navy to escort convoys of American supply ships and to shoot attacking German submarines on sight. He did so with the clear and accurate conviction that most Americans supported his policy. Yet he also nurtured that support by condemning German assaults on American destroyers without admitting that the submarines had been provoked. Certain that Congress was not prepared to declare war, he did not ask it to, though the most militant of his advisers wanted him to try. As they recognized, with the battle of the Atlantic underway he could not long pretend that he could keep war from America, but by the autumn of 1941, he appeared once again to be trapped, indecisively, between his personal and his political perceptions. The latter had stopped him short of the extraordinary presidential initiatives in foreign policy of Theodore Roosevelt—short, too, of implicating national prestige as Wilson had. Yet he now stood at the very edge of a war more portentous for the United States than any since the firing on Fort Sumter in 1861.

The trap sprung open only after Japan attacked Pearl Harbor. However wise or dangerous Roosevelt's policies in East Asia between 1939 and 1941, at no time did Congress seriously question either his authority or the manner in which he used it in that area. Then and later his critics held that he misjudged American interests. Actually he had several legitimate and persuasive concerns. The question of the "open door" interested him far less than it did the State Department, but he saw no way for the United States to condone the Japanese effort to conquer China. Beyond the immorality of that aggression, its success upset the balance of Pacific power, particularly after the Soviet Union had to deploy all its available force against the Germans in Europe. German advances in the west left the colonial possessions of other European powers vulnerable to Japan's announced plan for a "new order in Greater East Asia." The collapse of Holland and France, and the preoccupations of Great Britain reduced the obstacles to Japanese expansion in the Netherlands Indies, Indochina, and Malaysia. In the years after 1918 some nine or ten powers had interests in the southern and western Pacific which they were resolved to protect at least by negotiation; by late 1941, only the United States had the means to stand up to Japan. Yet Roosevelt, his priority fixed on the European war, hoped to avoid a showdown.

He failed because Japan would yield her intentions neither to American protests nor to American sanctions, tools unequal to their task. Late in 1940, after Japan joined the Rome-Berlin axis, the President placed an embargo on the export to Japan of high grades of gasoline and steel scrap. During successive crises the administration extended the embargo to cover lower grades of petroleum products and scrap, as well as aluminum and other materials essential to Japan and also to the American preparedness program. Meanwhile Roosevelt sent representatives to join discussions with the Dutch and British about the defense of the Pacific. In July 1941 the Japanese invaded Indochina, then a French colonial area. The President offered, if they would withdraw, to arrange a neutralization of the country and access for Japan to its raw materials. He also warned that the United States would help the Dutch if Japan moved against the Netherlands Indies, a rich source of rubber. Japanese silence signified, in the American interpretation, rejection of the offer and indifference to the warning. Roosevelt then froze all Japanese assets in the United States, a step preliminary to ending all commercial intercourse.

Japanese moderates responded with a request for direct negotiations at the highest level, but Roosevelt doubted they could control the military and, backed by Churchill, opposed what seemed to be Japan's minimum conditions. Those included a free hand in China and the immediate suspension of the American embargo. The President's decision not to negotiate in person worked to the advantage of the Japanese militants who gained control of the government in October 1941. While they secretly prepared for war, they restated the minimum conditions, but Roosevelt refused to abandon China. By insisting upon its independence, he demanded more than the United States could then guarantee.

Ultimately war came to the Pacific because the Japanese government, committed to its purposes, understood American opposition to them and believed it could prevail by starting a war it expected to win. American success in breaking the secret Japanese codes disclosed Japan's plans for a strike. The President and his advisers believed the Japanese would move south. Though they alerted all American forces in the Pacific, the bold Japanese attacks on Pearl Harbor, Guam, Wake Island, and the Philippines surprised both the troops stationed there, their commanders, and the President and his senior military staff. Following the disaster at Pearl Harbor on December 9, 1941, Germany and Italy declared war on the United States. The time of uncertainty was over. Roosevelt had not planned it that way. The costs of the surprise attack were enormous, especially to the navy he cherished. As he told the American people, "in the past few years—and, most violently in the past few days—we have learned a terrible lesson." The illusion of American isolation, of what Walter Lippmann later called "unearned security," had evaporated. It remained, as the President said, "to win the war and . . . the peace that follows." Particularly to the first of those goals he devoted his influence and his energy as long as he lived.

There was no possibility during the second world war for Roosevelt to do everything at once. Through most of 1942 the United States and its allies were losing the battle. In the Pacific the Japanese advanced eastward to Wake Island and south to the perimeters of Australia. In North Africa the Germans moved almost to Cairo, and in Russia to the outskirts of Moscow and Leningrad. Even during 1943 the counteroffensives of the united nations did not come nearly that close to Tokyo or Berlin, and almost half of 1944 passed before American forces reached Guam, before the Americans and British launched their invasion of Normandy, or before the Russians sent the Germans into a steady retreat.

During all those months of anguish, Roosevelt spoke on occasion about the ingredients of a peace, of an end not only to war but also to the beginning of war, and of his Four Freedoms—freedom from fear and want, freedom of speech and religion. But he was never a prophet, as Wilson had seemed to be. Constantly he was preoccupied by the war itself, with winning it as rapidly and as thoroughly as possible. Only victory, he believed, would bring the boys home and keep them there. Victory was his controlling priority, and to hasten and assure it, he did whatever he considered necessary. Not many Americans at that time questioned his choice or its consequences. So long as the fighting lasted, still fewer, in Congress or out, challenged his recourse to the extraordinary war powers of the presidency. With few exceptions Americans at arms or at home saw the Nazis as evil, as they were, the Japanese as perfidious, and both as brutal and dangerous foes to be defeated totally. Roosevelt had the support he needed for his view of the war and for the concessions to unconditional victory that he continually made.

At a press conference in December 1943, the President used a simple metaphor to illuminate the decision he had made two years earlier. "Dr. New Deal," a specialist in internal medicine, had been succeeded, he said, by an orthopedic surgeon, "Dr. Win-the-War." Roosevelt had neither seen nor considered any alternative to that change. He dared not alienate conservative Democrats whose votes he needed for his military and foreign policies. In coalition with the Republicans, they could still block social reform. Indeed after the Republican gains in the elections of 1942, the coalition set out to roll back the New Deal. Absorbed by the more exigent issues of war, Roosevelt had neither time nor strength much to resist. New ventures in reform, he believed, were bound to fail.

With substantial, often resounding public approval, Congress confirmed that assessment whenever he tested it. During 1943 Congress abolished all surviving relief agencies, ordered the dissolution of the only federal board engaged in long term economic planning—which the Republicans deemed socialistic, and pared appropriations for rural electrification and for assistance to agricultural workers. It also passed legislation directed against labor unions and held up the administration's revenue measure of 1943 which it passed in emasculated form early the next year. Grossly inadequate for national budgetary and economic needs, the revenue act contained new privileges for special interests. "It is . . . ," the President said in his veto message, "a tax relief bill . . . not for the needy but for the greedy." An angry Congress overrode the veto with majorities that included the Democratic leader of the Senate who resigned his post in protest against the President's action, only to assume it again after Roosevelt soothed his hurt feelings. In June 1944 the President yielded further to the temper of his party. Four years earlier he had insisted upon the nomination for vice-president of a leading Democratic liberal, Henry A. Wallace, then secretary of agriculture. Now he abetted the dumping of Wallace and the nomination instead of Senator Harry S Truman, a moderate from Missouri who suited the South and the city machines.

By 1944 the President had made much more serious sacrifices to the pursuit of victory. The procurement officers of the War and Navy Departments relied almost entirely upon the largest American firms which thrived as they never had before. It would have been inconvenient, but not impossible, to have channeled more business to their smaller competitors who were rapidly losing their share of market and corporate wealth. Worse, Henry L. Stimson, the aging secretary of war, confused his own racial prejudices, and those of his closest subordinates, with military necessity. Ordinarily the President allowed that confusion to prevail. So it was that the army continued to segregate American troops, only rarely to use black units in combat and then usually under the command of white officers, and only reluctantly and symbolically to assign black officers and men to flight duty. The navy was worse. Now and then, spurred by Mrs. Roosevelt or the complaints of black leaders, the President ordered a small correction of the Jim Crow practices of the armed services, but by and large he stood aside. Like Stimson, he doubted he could reform the army while also fighting a great war.

The President also subordinated civilian civil rights to convenience and to victory. Only to ward off a protest march on Washington that black leaders had organized, did he in 1941 establish the Fair Employment Practices Commission. He delegated responsibility for issues of importance to blacks, to members of his personal staff, or to officers in executive agencies. Though the manpower needs of industry sopped up black unemployment, American blacks suffered as they had so long from discrimination in hiring, schooling, and housing, and from the segregation of private facilities. Roosevelt seemed continually impatient with their efforts to alleviate their plight. During a war against Nazism and its racial doctrines, his administration did far less than it could have to combat racism within the United States.

In the name of necessity the President even condoned the most egregious violation of civil rights since the existence of slavery itself. Along the Pacific Coast prejudice against the Japanese reached hysterical proportions after the attack on Pearl Harbor. Though there was no evidence of serious disloyalty among Japanese immigrants, their children or grandchildren, and no authenticated instance of espionage or sabotage on their part, the army succumbed to the regional hatred and panic. "A Jap's a

Jap," the head of the West Coast Defense Command maintained. ". . . It makes no difference whether he is an American citizen or not. . . . There is no way to determine their loyalty." Stimson agreed. The "racial characteristics" of Japanese-Americans, he believed, "constituted a menace." With Roosevelt's consent, the army in 1942 evacuated Japanese-Americans from the western parts of the Pacific states and interned them in drab camps in the interior that were little better than prisons. There most of them remained throughout the war. The "whole policy," as one critic noted, was "headed . . . toward the destruction of constitutional rights . . . and . . . the establishment of racial discrimination as a principle of American government." It violated, as another critic said, "every democratic social value" and yet had the approval of "the Congress, the President and the Supreme Court." Then and later, no argument about the necessity for victory could in the least excuse it.

Only that kind of argument could begin to explain some of Roosevelt's controversial decisions about wartime foreign and military policy. The United States, for one example, had to keep China engaged in the war against Japan. The Chinese resistance held a large Japanese force on the mainland; Chinese troops were necessary for any major campaign against the Japanese in Burma; and until American advances in the Pacific provided a string of island bases, Chinese airfields seemed indispensable for the necessary bombing of the Japanese homeland. Yet China could be supplied only by treacherous flights over the Himalayas from India, and the weak, corrupt, and authoritarian Chinese Nationalist government of Chiang Kai-shek wasted much of the limited assistance it received. In spite of growing doubts about Chiang, Roosevelt retained more confidence in the possibility of influencing him than conditions warranted. Repeated efforts to persuade the Generalissimo to reform failed. The United States, the President believed, could not deliberately subvert Chiang's regime by supporting the Chinese Communist armies which were fighting both the Nationalists and the Japanese, nor could the United States undertake a full-scale land war in Asia. While Chiang staggered toward his own destruction, Roosevelt juggled command of American forces in China to prevent a rupture with him; yielded to most of his outrageous demands for American money; and tried to arrange an accommodation between him and his revolutionary opponents. Those tactics failed in all but their most urgent objective—China did not leave the war. Sentiment led the President to exaggerate the strength of the Nationalists, but unlike other Western statesmen, he also realized that a strong and independent China would occupy a powerful place in postwar world order.

In principle the President both expected and welcomed a gradual end to Western imperialism in Asia, including British India and French Indo-China. But Churchill, still unwilling to admit the erosion of British power, was devoted to the empire, and Roosevelt would not push him beyond the limits of their wartime collaboration. The two men continually exchanged concessions. On the issue of India, a problem for which the British had primary responsibility, Roosevelt retreated. He had no effective voice about Indo-China. He disliked Charles de Gaulle, the determined leader of the Free French, whose dedication to national grandeur had no match. Eventually de Gaulle received American military equipment, which he used with skill, but he also suffered reverses in his ambitions for himself and for France because of Roosevelt's doubts about his reliability and intentions. In his turn de Gaulle nourished both his resentment of the United States and his plans for French renaissance and imperial glory.

He had ample cause for his resentment. Following the fall of France in 1940, while de Gaulle was beginning to organize his forces of resistance from headquarters in London, the United States recognized the puppet Vichy regime which the Nazis used to govern the southern part of France, an area they did not immediately occupy. Instruments of German policy, Marshal Pétain and his collaborationist associates at Vichy adopted the fascist practices of their conquerors, fought against the British, and retaliated whenever they could against the growing French underground that despised them. Yet Roosevelt, in order to maintain at least a listening post in France, kept an American embassy at Vichy. Like de Gaulle, many American liberals considered that tactic a disgrace.

In 1942, at the time of the Anglo-American invasion of North Africa, the President approved an even more distasteful arrangement. His agents made a secret deal with Admiral Jean Darlan, a Vichyite notorious for his fascist sympathies. In return for signing an armistice a few days after the invasion began, Darlan received American recognition as the political chief in French North Africa. The armistice eased the campaign in Algeria and Morocco, but the recognition infuriated de Gaulle and stirred bitter protests in both England and the United States. Roosevelt excused his arrangement as "a temporary expedient, justified solely by the stress of battle," but he had, as his critics complained, conceded to a fascist. Though Darlan was assassinated soon thereafter, American civilian and military officials in North Africa continued to spurn de Gaulle, made little effort to terminate the anti-Semitic decrees earlier issued by Vichyites, and even invited to a senior local administrative office another unabashed fascist, Marcel Peyrouton.

That disheartening pattern prevailed again in Italy. After the successful Anglo-American attack on Sicily in 1943, Mussolini was forced to resign as head of the Italian government. The British and American commanders then began secret negotiations, endorsed by Churchill and Roosevelt, for an Italian surrender involving recognition of King Victor Emmanuel and his deputy, Marshal Pietro Badoglio, both fascists. The Allied negotiators expected their policy to speed Italian capitulation, bring them the

Italian navy, invite the cooperation of Italian soldiers and civilians, and embarrass German forces in Italy. They miscalculated. They got most of the navy, but the Germans, keeping the Italian people in a state of suppression, fought bitterly throughout the long, grueling Italian campaign. Most liberals in Europe, as well as many in the United States, deplored American recognition of the pompous little king and the beastly Badoglio. Expediency in Italy accomplished little of military value and raised understandable doubts about the genuineness of Roosevelt's tributes to freedom.

Secretary of War Stimson, a chief exponent of Mediterranean policy, and his senior associates in the War Department also continually tried to reduce or delay Lend-Lease allocations to the Soviet Union. They asserted again and again that American forces needed parts of the proposed shipments to build up their strength and to prepare for an invasion of Europe from England. However ingenuous that contention, it did not entirely mask the War Department's anxieties about Communism and suspicions of Russia.

About the issue of Lend-Lease for Russia Roosevelt was the genuine realist. He was resolved to prevent another Soviet accommodation with Hitler. Further, the Russians during 1942, 1943, and half of 1944 were carrying the brunt of the war in Europe, engaging millions of German troops, suffering and inflicting enormous losses. Victory depended upon their continuing intrepidity in the face of repeated Anglo-American delays in opening a second front in France. As the President put it in 1942, he wanted personally to see to it that nothing interfered with shipments promised the Soviet Union. "This is *critical*," he wrote, "because (a) we *must* keep our word (b) because Russian resistance counts *most* today." It continued to count, and he to keep his word. Partly in order to glue the Soviet Union to the wartime alliance, Roosevelt also persuaded Churchill to join his demand for unconditional surrender. But the President hedged his bets. Italian surrender was not unconditional. Lend-Lease shipments to the Soviet Union did not include some of the most advanced American weapons, and Russia was never officially informed about the Anglo-American development of the atomic bomb.

While American liberals were criticizing Roosevelt's dalliance with French and Italian fascists, American conservatives, the Republican leadership especially, condemned what they considered his concessions to Russia. Actually he gave the Soviet Union little it did not already have. He recognized that the United States could not force the Russians to withdraw from territory their troops had taken without starting a new war, an unthinkable eventuality. At the Yalta Conference of 1945 with Churchill and Stalin, he did solicit Russian participation in the war against Japan. His senior military commanders had advised him that they needed it; the atomic bomb had not then been produced or tested; and in any case, the United States had no means to prevent the Russians from the occupation of Asian areas into which they eventually moved. The President's major concessions went not to Stalin but to Churchill—to Churchill's repeated objections to the second front, to his refusal to open Palestine to Jewish refugees from Nazism, to his fanaticism about the British Empire.

More important, unlike his critics from the right, Roosevelt understood that after victory peace would depend not only on Anglo-American but also on Soviet-American amity. Perhaps he had a misplaced confidence in his personal influence with Stalin. Certainly he did not foresee, much less invite, the cold war. On the contrary, he planned after an armistice, rapidly and permanently to remove American forces from Europe, a course he expected public opinion to demand, as in 1945–46 it did. Thereafter he hoped to base postwar stability upon the continuing cooperation of his "four policemen," the United States, the United Kingdom, the Soviet Union, and China. Though Roosevelt died before he could complete or announce any specific plans, he seemed also to foresee a world order based on the domination of each of the great powers in its own region, a staged departure from colonialism, and at least a deliberative role for smaller nations—all within the framework of a United Nations. In that scheme, the smaller nations would have had less voice and perhaps fewer prerogatives than Woodrow Wilson had appeared to believe appropriate; the major powers, less unilateral authority than Theodore Roosevelt would have envisaged; and the United States, a shared responsibility for the preservation of world order and a special responsibility for both stability and good neighborliness in the Western Hemisphere.

After Roosevelt's death and after victory, those hopes crumbled. Like most of his contemporaries, Roosevelt had overestimated British strength and underestimated the economic distress of Europe and Asia, the aspirations of colonial peoples, and the mutual suspicions of governing authorities in Washington and Moscow. He had failed fully to appreciate that the American resort to Darlan and Badoglio, like the postponements of the second front, whetted Soviet anxieties, just as Russian seizures in the Baltic states and Eastern Europe confirmed British and American fears. Probably Roosevelt counted too much on his own ability to improvise once victory was won. He had no chance to try.

In the years before the war Roosevelt felt obliged to pursue simultaneously the goals of recovery and reform, incompatible though they sometimes became. During the war he made victory his overriding objective. That priority in the end entailed costs as large as those he incurred when his aim was less singular. Neither the human condition nor the nature of politics permitted any president to avoid the difficulty of serving one worthy end without damaging another desirable one. Just as both recovery and reform were necessary during the 1930s, so victory was essential in a total war. No action of Roosevelt's could have altered those circumstances. The actions he took proceeded in part from conditions he could not control—during the war not the least from limitations imposed by domestic politics and from the flexibility required for the preservation of an uneasy alliance. Yet however necessary, however arbitrary, some of Roosevelt's decisions impeded international comity and domestic social justice, causes he wanted to promote.

Early and late, the disparity between Roosevelt's expressed purposes and the results of his policies persuaded his most dogmatic critics, some from the right and some from the left, that he was a master of duplicity. He was not that. Rather, his choices on occasions entailed sacrifices perhaps less necessary than he let himself perceive. He was, after all, a statesman, not a prophet; a politician, not a professor; a president whose chosen role put a premium on doing. He disciplined his consciousness in order to protect his essential capacity to act from the complicating counsels of his democratic sympathies. Though not without miscalculations, he succeeded in peace and war in being his kind of liberal, his kind of conservative, his own best example of his firm belief that no fear was more crippling than the fear to act.

4

Lyndon Johnson and the Uncertain Legacy

IN BEHALF OF THE PROGRAMS he embraced as president, Lyndon Johnson exerted the extraordinary force of his person. As he put it himself: "I pleaded. I reasoned. I argued. I urged. I warned." The Johnson technique, honed earlier in his career, often overwhelmed its victims. "He moved in close," according to one observer, "his face a scant millimeter from his target, his eyes widening and narrowing, his eyebrows rising and falling. From his pockets poured clippings, memos, statistics. Mimicry, humor, and the genius of analogy made the Treatment an almost hypnotic experience and rendered the target stunned and helpless." And alarmed. In the judgment of Johnson's sympathetic biogra-

pher, "People felt they had no private space left in Johnson's presence. . . . The exercise of large power, the bending of other people's will to his, was a frightening thing to observe." Johnson
intended it to be. He wanted men around him, he once said
"who were loyal enough to kiss his ass in Macy's window and say
it smelled like a rose." He bellied his towering body up close to
the chests of physically smaller men; he mixed generosity and
rage, kindness and cruelty in order to dominate his office and
through it the government. The treatment provided only a super-
ficial measure of the man. In a crude but effective way, it substituted for the "animal energy" of Theodore Roosevelt, the eloquence of Woodrow Wilson, the wit and charm of FDR. As with
them, so with Johnson, manner was a significant weapon of policy. Johnson's policies derived from the legacy of reform as he
understood it. It was a heritage he meant to expand.

Lyndon Baines Johnson was born in 1908 near Johnson City
in southwest Texas. Though his family had a middling status in
the locality, he had only limited means as a boy, he felt the edges
of rural penury in his teens, and he worked his way through
Southwest Texas State Teachers College, the institution most
convenient for a young man seeking higher education in the
region of the Pedernales River. He taught high school only
briefly before leaving for Washington as the secretary of a Texas
Democratic congressman. Captured by the excitement of the
New Deal, Johnson returned to Texas to manage the state's
branch of the National Youth Administration, a responsibility he
discharged with both psychological and political reward. Elected
to the House of Representatives in 1937, he attached himself to
Sam Rayburn, the shrewd Texan who served for many years as
speaker, and to Franklin Roosevelt, whom Johnson viewed as a
patron rather more than the President saw him as a disciple. In
1948 he won election to the Senate after a close victory in the
primary. In the Senate he staked a shifting position just enough

to the left of his conservative southern colleagues to permit him to keep their trust while he also cultivated his more liberal brethren. In 1953 he became minority leader and in 1955, after the Democrats regained control of the Senate, majority leader, an office he enjoyed and mastered. By 1960 Johnson had more influence in Washington than did any other Democrat, a national reputation, a demonstrated capacity for leadership, and a hunger for the presidency. The preferred candidate of the South and of many conservative Democrats elsewhere, he lost the nomination to John F. Kennedy who selected him as his running mate partly because of Johnson's obvious abilities, partly because of his strength in southern states Kennedy needed to carry.

As Kennedy also realized, Johnson had a genuine concern for the poor and the proscribed. His memories of his own youth, his sensitivity to the needs of his rural neighbors, his continuing affection for the New Deal, and his vaulting view of American possibilities built his commitment to social reform beyond the limits of the prudential politics he had practiced during the preceding decade. Though he had absorbed much of the culture and manner of the "good ol' boys," Johnson was authentically democratic in his distaste for racial prejudice. He had managed the civil rights bills of the 1950's with a compelling sense of urgency and a precise calculation of possibility.

Kennedy's New Frontier operated with just that balance, but Johnson was not comfortable with his office or his environment. He was never content as a subordinate to any one. He also resented what he took to be a disdain for the South and for himself among Kennedy's circle of friends. He had deep reservations about the Ivy League background of Kennedy's intimates. Insecure in their company, he bolstered his courage by recourse to the macho vocabulary of the ranch, a language Kennedy also knew but used only in private. Johnson's more public vulgarity tended to confirm the suspicions of those who considered him gauche and also vain, devious, emotional, and egocentric. That assessment, partially valid, underestimated the political intelligence, social consciousness, and personal command of Lyndon Johnson.

His critics also underrated his understanding of the past and his anxiety about his place in history. He knew what the pattern of American reform had been, how much remained to be done, and how large was the role of the president in furthering change. Johnson had served in Congress during the long, dry season that began in 1939 and had yet to end in 1963. In that time a bloc of Republicans and of conservative Democrats, mostly southern, maintained a veto over reform legislation which they exercised with a tireless disregard for the fourth of a nation that needed help from the federal government. President Harry S Truman failed to achieve the goals of his Fair Deal partly because of his preoccupation with foreign policy, partly because of his lassitude in behalf of his program, but largely because of apathy on the Hill. His Republican successor, General Dwight D. Eisenhower, wanted to roll back the social gains of the 1930's. Indeed Johnson contributed far more than did Ike to the shaping of the admittedly inadequate Civil Rights Acts of 1957 and 1960, the signal reforms of the 1950's. John F. Kennedy developed a considerable agenda, his New Frontier, designed to attack poverty of all kinds, to stimulate the economy, and to erase discrimination against blacks. As late as 1963, however, the administration lacked the majorities in Congress necessary to effect those purposes which the conservative coalition still successfully blocked.

When Kennedy was assassinated in November 1963, Johnson immediately espoused Kennedy's program, in which he also believed. Though he shared the nation's shock and grief over the murder of the young President, he responded to his new office, as Theodore Roosevelt had, with a spontaneous sense of its possibilities. He had had twenty-three years in Congress where his prestige remained high. He had a remarkable knowledge of the federal government. He had an excellent personal staff and persuaded most of Kennedy's senior associates also to remain. And he had no doubts about the timeliness or significance of his objectives.

Johnson focused first on two measures, a revenue bill and a civil rights bill, so closely identified with Kennedy that a penitent Congress might grant him in death what it had denied him in life. The revenue bill proposed a tax reduction in order to encourage investment and spur economic growth. A resulting increase in national income would lift federal revenues sufficiently to support poverty-related programs. Kennedy's advisers, adherents of the new economics derived from J. M. Keynes, even gave up the possibility of tax reform for the sake of their stimulative bill. But the business community and conservatives in Congress did not trust the New Frontiersmen who struck them as latter-day New Deal spenders. In contrast, Johnson spoke the language of prudence. He "spread the word," he later recalled, that he would pare the budget so as to reduce the projected deficit from $9 billion to $5 billion. By appearing the champion of fiscal responsibility, he won enough confidence on the Hill to put the tax bill across. It produced the anticipated economic effects. It also eased the taxes of both the wealthy and the middle class, of both big business and smaller enterprise, with the calculable result of enhancing Johnson's standing with those groups. He had made prudence and prosperity his issues for 1964 and built an enlarged constituency for the rest of his program.

The civil rights bill, central to that program, had emerged from Kennedy's increasing responsiveness to the momentum of the civil rights movement. By 1963 the leadership of that movement centered in Dr. Martin Luther King, Jr., the extraordinary black minister whose courage, eloquence, and tactical virtuosity had made him an American Gandhi. Continual confrontations between King's followers, black and white devotees of civil disobedience, and the public custodians of southern segregation had given a growing urgency to King's great cause. As chairman of Kennedy's Committee on Equal Employment Opportunity, Johnson said, he had again come "face to face with the deep-seated discrimination" that obstructed the employment and the education of blacks. "In the spring of 1963," he later wrote, "events in Birmingham, Alabama, showed the world the glaring contrast between the restraint of the black demonstrators and the brutality of the white policemen." King's March on Washington that summer further moved the nation. For Johnson, as he continued, nothing made "a man come to grips more directly with his conscience than the Presidency. . . . The burden of his responsibility literally opens up his soul. . . . So it was with me . . . I would use every ounce of strength I possessed to gain justice for the black Americans."

To that end Johnson put his prestige as president behind Kennedy's civil rights bill which was designed to end segregation in public restaurants and hotels. If southern Democratic senators, assisted as they had so often been by Republicans, could prevent cloture, they could threaten a filibuster in order to force a weakening of the measure. Johnson cut off that possibility. He had an easy familiarity with his former colleagues in the Senate that Kennedy had lacked. Using that advantage, he made it clear to the senior southerners that he would accept no compromise. He also brought his powerful treatment to bear upon the minority leader, Republican Senator Everett Dirksen, whose vanity the President engaged in behalf of the bill. Dirksen, previously opposed to several aspects of the measure, enjoyed his unusual role as a champion of democracy. Among Senate liberals, Hubert H. Humphrey, operating according to Johnson's prescriptions, established a disciplined emphasis on dignified bipartisanship. With the liberals moderating their rhetoric and enough Republicans faithful to Dirksen, a motion for cloture failed. That killed the chance of a filibuster and assured the passage of the Civil Rights Act of 1964. It ended legal discrimination in public places, in employment, and in voter registration, and it authorized the attorney general to institute suits in behalf of injured individuals. Addressed, like earlier acts, more against conditions in the South than in the North, it was nevertheless the strongest measure of its kind to that date, and a major triumph for Johnson.

In January 1964 the President had called for "unconditional war on poverty in America." His program owed most of its substance to the planning of the Kennedy administration which had addressed the special problems of the aged and the ill, and of the untrained and unemployed in Appalachia and in urban slums. Johnson sponsored refined versions of those plans in a distinctive personal style which he associated with the late nineteenth-century populism of his native Southwest. Again with consummate skill, he shepherded through Congress the Economic Opportunity Act of 1964 which authorized $750 million for jobs and training, for the support of community efforts to attack poverty, and for creating a domestic social service corps modeled upon Kennedy's overseas Peace Corps and described by a new acronym, VISTA, "Volunteers in Service to America." The act also enabled the establishment of the Head Start program for disadvantaged preschool children and the Upward Bound program for poor but aspirant collegians. Though Republicans forced Congress to table the administration's proposal for national medical insurance, that important reform obviously awaited only the President's re-election.

Johnson yearned for election in his own right. He later recalled hesitations born of his self-consciousness as a southerner, his resulting fear that the country would not accept his leadership, and his worry about his health—though it had been excellent since a serious heart attack nine years earlier. In fact he had no real doubts. He believed he would become the greatest of presidents and he wanted the job desperately. Consequently he rejoiced in his strategy as well as his achievements. He had obtained civil rights legislation without alienating the South or its representatives. His poverty program scored points with the eastern liberals whose regard he privately valued. The coalitions he had put together on the Hill foreshadowed the construction he had begun of a "consensus" so broad that he could achieve election by an overwhelming majority. Apart from blacks, and white liberals, usually conservative Democrats praised the tax reduction, as did much of the business community, which was prospering as the economy boomed and reconciled to a poverty program in which corporations were to play an altruistic but potentially profitable part. Indeed in contrast to Roosevelt in 1936, Johnson in 1964 cultivated the managers of American industry, a marked departure from previous liberal practice. Outside of the President's fold stood only inveterate Republicans, adamant southern segregationists, and a still small corpus of blue-collar whites disgruntled by the gains of the blacks and the poor.

Perhaps as much because of his confidence as because of his simmering jealousy, Johnson excluded one potentially powerful man, Attorney General Robert F. Kennedy, a younger brother and the intimate disciple of the late President. Johnson and Kennedy had long resented each other. Johnson believed, not without cause, that Robert Kennedy had opposed his selection as vice-president, that Kennedy had little respect for him, that Kennedy and his friends were trying to hold center stage. "He never liked me," Johnson said, "and that's nothing compared to what I think of him." Though Kennedy had stayed on as attorney general, effective in his office but now remote from the White House, he felt that Johnson had been callous in his behavior after the assassination and given John Kennedy small credit for his large contributions to the achievements of 1964.

The clash came over Johnson's choice of a vice-president. Kennedy thought about that office though he never declared his candidacy. He knew that Johnson did not want him, but he was unwilling to accommodate the President by dropping out of contention, and he was resolved to remain in public life. Johnson thought he was campaigning. The President stopped it in July 1964 by announcing that he deemed it "inadvisible . . . to recommend . . . [for vice-president] any member of the cabinet." He had already told Kennedy about that decision which incidentally eliminated several others unacceptable to the President. Later Johnson made the implausible statement that he had to keep the cabinet from campaigning in order to prevent government business from coming to a halt. As it worked out, Kennedy ran successfully for United States senator from New York, a position from which he enhanced his stature, and Johnson, after teasing a number of aspirants, picked Hubert Humphrey, whose promises of personal loyalty and whose impeccable liberal credentials seemed to make him on all accounts a satisfactory choice.

Meanwhile the Republicans guaranteed Johnson's victory by nominating Senator Barry Goldwater of Arizona as their candidate. An easily likeable man, Goldwater had a slack intelligence which suffused his political declaration of 1960, *The Conscience of a Conservative*. In that book or in his campaign speeches, Goldwater, who believed that active government endangered freedom, called on various occasions for the abolition of the income tax, the sale of the Tennessee Valley Authority, and the reduction or elimination of Social Security. In the world as it had become, it was he who seemed radical, for his program, in so far as it was comprehensible, threatened to rip apart the social fabric that decades of intermittent reform had knit. In that context, his statement in his acceptance speech that "extremism in the defense of liberty is no vice," alarmed most Americans who thereafter perceived Johnson as the moderate in the race. The President managed to place himself in that position also on issues of foreign policy. He benefited further from the rough tactics of the Goldwater forces at the Republican convention which infuriated less reactionary members of the party, of whom many swung over to Johnson. After an acerbic but dull campaign, Johnson pulled over 60 percent of the popular vote and carried forty-four states, while the Democrats rolled up commanding majorities in the House and Senate—a victory unequalled since Roosevelt's landslide in 1936.

During the campaign Johnson had talked continually about the "Great Society"—his New Deal, his New Frontier—which he had first begun to describe the previous May. It included the war against poverty and the struggle for racial equality, and, as he said in his inaugural address in 1965, it also asked "not only how much, but how good; not only how to create wealth, but how to use it; not only how fast we are going, but where are we headed. It proposes as the first test of a nation: the quality of its people." In order to fulfill the needs of the spirit, he said, the nation had first to establish freedom from the wants of the body. He urged Congress to do both, to beautify the country, eliminate water and air pollution, clean up the cities, provide medical care for the aged and education for the young, and guarantee voting rights to blacks still ordinarily barred from the polls in the South. Those objectives grew out of Franklin Roosevelt's Economic Bill of Rights of 1944, now expanded, and they projected forward the agenda of gradualistic reform—"the American dream" in the phrase of one of Johnson's biographers—at a time propitious for its achievement.

Johnson had the votes in Congress, the skill to muster them and the weight of public opinion on his side. Spurred by the President, Congress passed the medical act which provided $6.5 billion for Medicare under Social Security for all Americans 65 or over and Medicaid, supported by federal grants to the states, to furnish special help to the poor. Another $23 billion went for economic development of the Appalachian region and for slum clearance and the creation of model urban communities. Still other funds met Johnson's remaining requests. There was more to come, for he had soaring aspirations for the United States. He meant to nurture the quality of American life through the expansion of federal authority, by regulation as well as by appropriation, to set standards for healthy natural and urban environments, for the protection of consumers against fraud and deceit, and for the cultivation of the arts and humanities. He looked forward, he said, to a civilization "where the demands of morality, and the needs of the spirit, can be realized in the life of the nation." Though that was a task for at least two generations, he attempted characteristically to dispatch it in two years. He was hurried, everywhere at once, prone to confuse first measures with ultimate success. His claims were exaggerated, his poses transparent, his tears contrived, but his enormous energy produced impressive results. His record in 1965–66 rivaled those of Wilson in 1913–14 and Roosevelt in 1935.

Two of Johnson's proposals, one for elementary education, the other to protect the right to vote, again demanded his special political agility. Kennedy had lost his aid-for-education bill partly because the hierarchy of the Catholic church, his church, fought federal assistance for public schools in the absence of similar assistance for parochial schools. The bill also met conventional congressional and public antipathy for supporting education on any but a local basis. Johnson neutralized both sources of opposition. On the advice of one of his task forces, he suggested providing federal aid for elementary and secondary schools not on a general basis but according to a selective formula which took into account both the poverty of the school district and the amount of the state's average educational expenses per child. Johnson's bill also required each school district to make available special educational services, such as textbooks and television, to children in private and parochial, as well as public schools. That provision satisfied Catholics and funding by direct grants to the states reassured those fearful of federal intrusion in the schools. The President also deployed official ambassadors to special interest groups.

"Slowly," he recollected, "in curious ways, opposition melted." The Elementary and Secondary Education Act of 1965, which Johnson signed in the one-room schoolhouse he had first attended, provided $1.3 billion for the school systems it reached. It was the first of a series of acts of the Johnson administration that assisted schools, libraries, colleges and universities. As one consequence, higher education for five years enjoyed the sunniest season it had ever known.

In 1965 Johnson gave highest priority to the voting rights bill which he had ordered his Justice Department to draft. He believed, as did thousands of liberal Americans, that univ̇ersal suffrage for blacks, in the South as well as North, would give them the means through politics to promote their own welfare. The southern states had effectively disfranchised blacks for seven decades. Leaders of the largest civil rights organizations were stressing the importance of removing that barrier. In 1965 Martin Luther King, Jr., directed a dramatic demonstration for the cause, a march to proceed from Selma to Montgomery, Alabama. At the outskirts of Selma, state troopers battered the marchers who had refused their order to turn back. Some fifty demonstrators suffered injuries. Several days later a group of white vigilantes murdered a white Boston clergyman, a "nigger lover" in their obscene explanation. The bruality of the episodes, caught in part by television cameras, reached millions of American homes and provoked a national demand for the use of federal troops to protect King and his company. With that sentiment behind him, Johnson maneuvered the governor of Alabama into admitting he could not afford to mobilize the National Guard, a confession that permitted the President to federalize the Alabama guard under his command and order it to defend the right of the marchers to proceed peacefully to their destination.

The national mood, as King had intended, also supported the voting rights bill. While again working on Everett Dirksen, Johnson addressed Congress on behalf of the measure. "I speak tonight," he began, at his oratorical best, "for the dignity of man and the destiny of democracy. . . . There is no issue of state's rights. . . . There is only the struggle for human rights. . . . Even if we pass this bill, the battle will not be over. . . . The effort of American Negroes to secure for themselves the full blessings of American life . . . must be our cause, too. Because . . . it is all of us who must overcome the crippling legacy of bigotry and injustice. And—we—shall—overcome."

Those three last words, the refrain of the hymn which Martin Luther King, Jr., had made his anthem, reflected Johnson's unstinting commitment to the issue. To his gratification, the Voting Act of 1965, which Congress passed in August, eliminated discriminatory literacy tests, provided federal officers to assist black voter registration, and established severe penalties for interference with an individual's right to the ballot. It set in motion, for the first time in a century, the rapid inclusion of blacks in the southern electorate. Yet as Johnson observed at the Howard University commencement, it was not enough: "We seek not just freedom but opportunity. We seek not just . . . equality as a right and a theory but equality as a fact and a result."

For that grand but distant objective, the President counted on his various poverty programs. In the years 1965 to 1970, those programs received $10 billion in appropriations. Together with the growth of the economy, the distributive impact of federal policies lifted half the Americans who had been below the poverty line above that mark. Blacks especially but not exclusively participated in those advances. Because prejudice and poverty did not by any means disappear, it became fashionable in later years to dismiss Johnson's Great Society as a failure, to belittle his efforts by asserting that the nation could not solve problems by throwing money at them. Those were charges born of reactionary convenience. The Great Society, to be sure, promised too much and delivered too little. There was waste and misdirection and inefficiency. But the fault lay primarily in inadequate spending for too short a period, as well as in the administrative confusion that characterized Johnson's presidency. More orderly, more sustained and more generous attention to his objectives would have brought them closer to realization. Even as it was, between 1963 and 1969 blacks made substantial gains in employment, income, education, and health, as well as in access to public facilities and to the vote. In the same period the poor in general benefited from federal support for child care, medical care, low income housing, job training, and community action organized for widespread participation. Johnson had cause to boast about his record.

The hurdles on which Johnson stumbled stood primarily outside of the processes of legislation and appropriation. They involved for the most part the uncertainties that had beset his progressive predecessors. By 1965 they had become protuberant. Johnson's style of administration, for one factor, raised anew the old question of the role of an elite in democratic government. In one sense, he ranged far beyond Theodore Roosevelt and Wilson, beyond FDR, in the recruitment of his senior associates. Personal wealth, religion, family background, section, and now even race did not count in Johnson's determination of eligibility. As a matter of policy, not just as a token, he selected able blacks for major offices, for two outstanding examples, Robert E. Weaver as secretary of the new Department of Housing and Urban Affairs, and Thurgood Marshall as associate justice of the Supreme Court. Johnson also expected his reforms soon to swell the number of qualified blacks and other minorities.

Yet in another sense, he restricted his important appointments, as he had to, to the small minority of Americans qualified to undertake the increasingly technical and complex duties of public office. By 1963 there was diminishing room within government for amateurs or generalists. Even lawyers, the versatile entrepreneurs of the New Deal, now needed to operate often on the basis of specialized learning and experience. Like Kennedy before him, Johnson recognized the need to recruit a new class of experts for the expanding business of government. The Great Society programs depended for execution largely on university trained professionals, lawyers of course, but also economists, sociologists, scientists, publicists, and at lesser but still significant levels of authority, technicians in all relevant callings. Those men and women represented no special caste or class. They were learned and ambitious, a self-conscious core of talent available alike to government, business, and the academy. They were also a recognizable elite. They did not identify with "the common man." Like the public-spirited patricians of the early century and the inventive plebians of the New Deal, they put a high value on power and status. They expected, if they entered government, to exercise a genuine authority over their assigned domains, and they expected to have their orders obeyed. There was no populism in them.

Johnson's obsession with his own power often frustrated his subordinates. The President felt threatened by proposals he did not generate and by juniors he could not control. He deliberately jumbled the jurisdictions of the members of his personal staff so that he could cut off the initiatives of those who seemed adventurous beyond his skittish tolerance. By limiting the access of his staff to the media, he reserved for himself the place in the sun of television and the press. He was so much resolved to make the news himself that a published leak of a pending appointment sufficed to provoke him to cancel it. He bruised his assistants by lavishing praise or gifts on a man one day, then berating him or ostracizing him the next. His volatile moods created anxieties in his White House like those of a tense child with unpredictable parents. Most of the ablest of the Kennedy staff who remained to serve Johnson, many of the ablest of his own, sooner or later resigned, wounded and exhausted by the President's ways.

So too with the cabinet. As Johnson admitted, "I was determined to turn those lordly men into good soldiers . . . to make them more dependent on me than I was on them." Through his control over the budget and over liaison with Congress, he increased the dominance of the White House over the executive departments. The President ordered the cabinet members to send the reports of their task forces only to him. He seemed to take special pleasure in dangling a cabinet or subcabinet appointment before an aspirant for so long that an eager candidate had to beg for it. As he told one cabinet wife, with obvious pride, all her counterparts and their husbands were afraid of him.

Johnson's grandiosity crippled government. His insistence on supreme command made the White House the sole arbiter of departmental rivalries for funds and authority. The resulting bureaucratic confusions persisted while his own aides dared not decide an issue without his approval, and while he, in spite of his energy, could not, or often wantonly would not address the matter. As one consequence, the programs of the Great Society faltered. Standards for clear water, clear air, and urban redevelopment had to be promulgated, but the proliferation of regulatory offices generated conflicting orders and the hodgepodge of authority magnified those conflicts to the point of disarray. The dissatisfactions of the specialists brought to Washington grew in tandem with the resentments of managers subject to regulation. Both became dubious about the capacity of the federal government properly to use its growing power. Johnson was creating a personal leviathan beyond any man's ability to manage. Administration, "the bulk of government," depended upon responsible, disinterested experts, but Johnson's manner undermined even the best and the brightest of them.

Demanding total loyalty from his subordinates, as he did, Johnson asked about as much from the American people. Though he liked to think of himself as a populist, he dismissed criticism of his policies as ignorant or malicious. By 1965 dissent had emerged among urban blacks in the North, whose gratitude Johnson expected. The civil rights movement had mostly affected the South. In northern cities, blacks suffered still, as they always had, from segregation in housing and schooling and from discrimination in employment, as well as from inferior incomes and from the debilitation of morale inherent in ghetto life. The missionary Christianity of Martin Luther King, Jr., and his doctrines of peaceful protest had a limited appeal to a new generation of urban black leaders whose anger over their lot mounted to a rage against whites. By the mid-1960's a powerful black nationalism, often blatantly radical, was sweeping cities with large black populations, among them Los Angeles, Detroit, Newark, Chicago, Washington, and New York. In 1965 riots in Watts, the black section of Los Angeles, were subdued by the National Guard only after 34 deaths and $35 million of property damage. Within a year the militants among blacks were demanding not just "black power" but also reparation and retaliation, and were calling for violence as an instrument of change.

Like most whites and many, perhaps most blacks, Johnson abhorred that development. He attempted to combat it by moving along familiar lines, which his successful proposal for a federal open-housing law represented. But traditional means of redress carried no conviction for the militants who disowned the very system the President was trying to improve. Johnson, for his part, could not believe that black Americans were resisting his leadership. Though he recognized the continuing aggravations of poverty and discrimination, he also repaired to the questionable assumption that the black majority had faith in him, that basically agitators were causing the trouble. Most of the elite around him, including the leaders of the older black organizations, shared Johnson's conviction that they knew best how to help black Americans and that most blacks wanted them to. Certainly their policies had merit. Probably they were correct in their head count. But their assessment did not accurately measure the urban mood. Intensity, in the circumstances, mattered as much or more than numbers. Johnson had endorsed the participatory principles of community action programs; he rejected the product of participation when it challenged his policies or power. Like liberals in the past, he could not entirely reconcile his belief in elite government, in his case in almost a singular elite, with his professions of majoritarianism; he could not find a place for radical dissent within his meliorative doctrines. He had not invented those problems, but neither did he solve them.

Only on the surface did he dispel yet another ambiguity of American reform. As he saw it, the consensus he had cultivated for the Great Society enlisted industrialism and its corporate managers in the quest for a better quality of life, and placed the energy of rising productivity in the service of the values of beauty, grace and humanity. Like many of his generation, he was premature in that conclusion, for he was counting on economic growth to increase the resources he intended to distribute to deserving people and worthy ends. Yet that growth entailed a quickening depletion of finite sources of physical energy, which in itself threatened the quality of the environment he wanted to enhance. The tension of the early century between a longing for a bucolic past and a craving for the affluence of an industrial future, the tension of the New Deal between the rationalizers and the antitrusters, expressed itself in the 1960's in the tension between growth and quality, between energy and environment.

Apart from the problem of growth, the support Johnson had generated among business managers and within the middle class rested in part on their prosperity, the continuing increase in their real income, an income produced in part by Johnson's fiscal policy and protected by the near absence of inflation. Any substantial increase in corporate and personal income taxes, any drift into inflation, would bring on a disenchantment among the relatively affluent as serious as the expanding backlash of blue-collar Americans against the black and the poor. The priorities of the Great Society and of the political consensus behind it had an importance that Johnson could ill afford to neglect. Yet by 1965 his foreign and military policies were drawing him into a mire from which he could not escape without recourse to the taxes or to the inflation he had to avoid. By that time those policies had also begun to expose, more starkly than had domestic events, the flaws in his personal style, the problems of elite government, the significance of intensity as against number in reading the public mood, and the danger of a presidency deliberately and increasingly insulated from criticism, pluralism, and accountability.

Less experienced, less informed, less confident about foreign than about domestic policy, Lyndon Johnson felt the need for experts to instruct him, though he decided what advice to take, and to identify his administration with a lineage of acceptable conventionality. So it was that in his memoir he stressed his own contributions to his domestic triumphs, often to the neglect of the initiatives of other presidents, but in discussing his ventures abroad, he continually defended them as extensions of the decisions of Kennedy, Eisenhower, Truman and even sometimes Roosevelt. Like his advisers, Johnson believed he was following in the steps of his predecessors, and he did not question the wisdom of their course. Before 1963 relatively few Americans did. Between the parties and among candidates for national office, there were disagreements about tactics and emphasis in foreign policy, but a common interpretation about the cold war and the need to wage it prevailed alike in Washington and the hinterland.

The legacy of doctrine Johnson accepted derived at least from the time of Harry S Truman, though its roots went back to the concern of the two Roosevelts to nurture a balance of power in both Europe and Asia that would prevent a potential enemy of the United States from dominating either continent and from challenging American hegemony in the Western Hemisphere. With the end of World War II, Truman and his counselors perceived such an enemy in the Soviet Union. The strongest military presence in both Europe and Asia, the Soviet Union during and immediately after the war expanded its frontiers westward, gained control over Eastern and Central Europe, occupied Manchuria, and stepped up the flow of its support to the revolution in China. With the success of that revolution, China emerged as an ally—as seen from Washington, even a satellite, of Moscow. The world situation, in the interpretation of Presidents Truman and Eisenhower, as also Lyndon Johnson, resembled that of 1940, with Russia rather than Germany now threatening Western Europe and the Atlantic, with China rather than Japan now threatening Asia and the Pacific, and with communism rather than fascism now providing a doctrinal danger to democratic government.

From those perceptions flowed the policies of containment of the Truman and Eisenhower years—the policies that rebuilt the Western European economy, rearmed West Germany, forged the North Atlantic Alliance, underlay the war in Korea, animated the regional defense treaties negotiated for Southeast Asia and other areas, built the national military establishment and its atomic arsenal, and inspired American military and economic aid to developing nations. Through those policies the United States was endeavoring, with considerable effect, to restrict the sphere of Soviet and Chinese influence everywhere in the world.

Truman had announced that purpose in his celebrated doctrine which called for American assistance for any country endangered by Communist aggression or subversion. The universalism of that doctrine troubled some critics, as did the assumption that the United States had the means to carry out the extraordinary mission Truman proclaimed. So, too, Truman failed to take into account the degree to which postwar American policies provoked, however inadvertently, Soviet responses. Further, in a measure then not yet as obvious as it became, the Soviet Union and China were not inexorably linked, and among the peoples of Africa and Asia, indigenous nationalism, whether or not dressed in Communist rhetoric, constituted in itself a powerful force directed against Western colonial rule, a force independent of Russian or Chinese subversion. But those considerations paled in the official and the public mind against the backdrop of Soviet militarism, evidence of Soviet espionage in the United States and elsewhere, and the resulting American hysteria about a Communist conspiracy at home and abroad. Even after that panic subsided, the remaining suspicions of Russia and China vitiated opposition within the United States to the continuing cold war and its attendant strategies.

In those years Johnson, a major influence in the Senate, continually stood behind Truman and Eisenhower. In 1960 he agreed with the stress in Kennedy's campaign on increased American preparedness as a deterrent to Soviet aggression. As vice-president he took no basic exception to Kennedy's conduct of foreign affairs, though he favored tougher tactics toward Communist Cuba than Kennedy did, and he had fewer reservations about some of the authoritarian regimes which the United States was sponsoring. After Kennedy's assassination, Johnson announced his commitment to Kennedy's politics and asked Kennedy's senior advisers on foreign affairs to carry on in the White House, the State Department, the Defense Department, and the Central Intelligence Agency. Like Kennedy and like Johnson, they were the inheritors of fifteen years of the cold war, and they shared a confident conviction in the wisdom and beneficence of American intentions and the indispensability of American power and the will to use it.

Common assumptions about American foreign policy did not yield total agreement within Johnson's councils. As had Kennedy, so did Johnson receive conflicting advice about particular issues as they arose. No one could be certain of what Kennedy might have decided about the changing circumstances within the various areas of American interest. Consequently Johnson could not in any exact sense follow Kennedy's track, though he continually asserted that he did. In general that claim held true for Europe, though Johnson was more conciliatory toward French President Charles de Gaulle than Kennedy had been. In Asia there was room for more doubt. In Latin America, Johnson preserved at the most only a semblance of Kennedy's program.

Latin America had been the stepchild of American foreign policy during the Truman and Eisenhower years. Preoccupied with Europe and Asia, Washington directed little economic assistance to the countries of the Western Hemisphere, interceded now and then to provide clandestine help to governments—no matter how undemocratic—loyal to American leadership, supported those governments with stocks of obsolete American arms, and ignored the growing poverty and misery and resentment of most of the people in the area. Surprised by the Castro revolution in Cuba, the Eisenhower administration attributed its success largely to Russian involvement rather than popular anger with a corrupt and dictatorial ancien régime.

Kennedy knew better. Resolved to limit Russian military power in Cuba and Cuban influence in the Americas, he realized that the latter objective required a return to Franklin Roosevelt's Good Neighbor policy. To that end his Alliance for Progress employed American economic assistance to promote democratic reform. He looked forward to a decade of cooperative effort to stimulate economic growth and lift standards of living, an effort that would involve substantial changes, "a peaceful revolution," in Latin American social structure.

The Alliance for Progress impressed Johnson much less than did Kennedy's direct relations with Cuba. In 1961 Kennedy approved a plan formulated under Eisenhower for an invasion of the island by anti-Castro expatriates trained and assisted by the CIA. When their landing at the Bay of Pigs collapsed, the President refused to send in American reinforcements whose arrival might have turned the day but would surely have signaled the start of a war. The episode drew criticism from those who lamented the attempt and from those who condemned the failure. Johnson came to take the latter point. When he reached the presidency, he was determined not to lose another Cuba, nor, as Roosevelt and Truman had been accused of doing, another China. The Bay of Pigs, he concluded, had diminished Kennedy's stature with the Russians and encouraged their ambitions in Europe and the Caribbean. In 1962 the Soviet Union began to build bases in Cuba for nuclear missiles pointed toward the United States. During the ensuing crisis, Kennedy, risking war, demanded the removal of the missiles, to which Moscow acceded. As Johnson read the outcome, it taught the necessity for toughness with the Soviet Union and for preclusive action to prevent any Caribbean country from moving into the Cuban or Russian orbit.

The Alliance for Progress did not suit Johnson's purpose. The prospect of "peaceful revolution" endangered a number of autocratic regimes he wanted to hold to American policy. Further, American business, accustomed to working with those regimes, preferred them to the uncertain alternatives social reform might establish. While continuing to supply economic assistance, Johnson abandoned the social and political goals of the Alliance. He indicated that change with his appointment in 1964 of Thomas Mann as assistant secretary of state for hemispheric affairs. A confirmed colonialist and a Texan scornful of Latins, Mann had a zealous regard for commercial interests. He suspended aid to the democratic government of Peru in an attempt to force its submission to the terms of an American oil company. He won Johnson's quick recognition for a reactionary military coup in Brazil. And he encouraged Johnson's revival of the gunboat diplomacy of Theodore Roosevelt.

In 1963 the military in Santo Domingo had overthrown the ineffectual but democratic government of Juan Bosch. Allied with some aggrieved officers and more impatient patriots of the left, Bosch's supporters struck back in the spring of 1965. Johnson interpreted the ensuing fracas as a function of Castro's influence. "We don't propose to sit here," he said, ". . . and let the Communists set up any government in the Western Hemisphere." On the pretext of protecting American lives and restoring order, he sent some 22,000 marines, far more than his pretext excused, into Santo Domingo. Through his representatives he then blocked the installation of a temporary government under Bosch, whom he labeled an extremist, a fatuous charge. Johnson had proceeded initially without consulting the Organization of American States. He later complained that the size and emotionalism of that body kept it from acting decisively, though it did endorse his action after the fact. As he put it with his macho nuance, the OAS "couldn't pour piss out of a boot if the instructions were written on the heel." Johnson's course and his attitudes offended liberals in Santo Domingo and throughout Latin America. He renewed anxieties about the Yankee colossus and discouraged democrats eager for social change. As one disconsolate Mexican remarked, the Alliance for Progress was dead.

In all but name, Johnson had departed from Kennedy's policy in Latin America. In so doing he troubled many who had been in the late President's camp, Robert Kennedy in particular. Others of John Kennedy's former staff served as Johnson's agents in Santo Domingo. Whatever the merit of Johnson's decisions, he had his quota of Ivy League experts to defend them. It was not a matter of experts, for experts disagreed. Nor was it a matter of continuity or discontinuity. The issue was one of Johnson's judgment. Adlai Stevenson, ambassador to the United Nations, twice the defeated Democratic candidate for president, elder statesman of the party's liberals, raised the telling question: "When I consider what the administration did in the Dominican Republic," he said, "I begin to wonder if we know what we are doing in Vietnam."

American involvement in Vietnam had grown for a decade before Johnson became president. Under Truman and Eisenhower American weapons sent to France made their way to French forces fighting in Vietnam against the movement for independence led by Ho Chi Minh. Eisenhower considered the defeat of that movement one objective of the Southeast Asia Treaty which he negotiated with six other nations, though the terms of the agreement did not mandate action by any one of the signatories. With the expulsion of the French and the division of Vietnam, Washington became the chief sponsor of the South Vietnam government in Saigon, allegedly a democratic but actually a despotic regime allied to the West. The United States supported that government in its refusal to cooperate in a national election which would have resulted in a predicted victory for Ho Chi Minh. His Communist government in Hanoi in North Vietnam still strove to unite the whole country under its rule and collaborated to that end with guerilla groups in the south. In the American view, that effort was part of the worldwide Communist threat. Russian supplies were reaching Ho Chi Minh. Spokesman for national independence though he was, he was also admittedly a Communist, and contrary to some American fancies, a dictatorial ruler capable, like Stalin and like Mao, of ruthlessness and cruelty. Those qualities served to sustain Washington's dubious argument that the United States was fostering democracy through its commitment to South Vietnam.

Actually that commitment originated partly in the mistaken belief that Ho Chi Minh was subservient to Russia and China, and from the application to Asia of the fallacious domino theory which had once supposed that the loss of independence in Latvia would open all Europe to the red tide. Recast by Eisenhower, that proposition held that "the loss of South Vietnam would set in motion a crumbling process that could . . . have significance for us and for freedom." Kennedy had agreed that Vietnam was key to a necessary western presence in the area. Johnson, while still vice-president, carried the warning further. "If we don't stop the Reds in South Vietnam," he predicted, "tomorrow they will be in Hawaii, and next week they will be in San Francisco."

With equal implausibility, Johnson, while on an inspection trip to Saigon for Kennedy, called President Ngo Dinh Diem of South Vietnam the Churchill of Southeast Asia. Diem was at least as brutal as Ho Chi Minh, withal corrupt and largely despised among the people he ruled. As an agent of American policy he embarrassed Kennedy who in 1963 permitted American cooperation with South Vietnamese generals in their overthrow of Diem, whom they also murdered. None to be preferred to Diem, those generals took over in Saigon only soon to fall to another coup. Johnson had serious reservations about American involvement in the conspiracy against Diem. Then and later, his indifference to the personal integrity and popular support of American puppets in Saigon compromised his repeated contentions about defending democracy. If Kennedy had lived, he might have behaved identically, but as in Santo Domingo, the issue was not continuity, as Johnson so often argued, but judgment. Once president, Johnson did not question the general premises of his predecessors about Vietnam. Rather, he followed the lines of policy they had drawn because he believed in them. He subscribed, too, to their parlous metaphor identifying British appeasement of Hitler in 1938 with any accommodation with Ho Chi Minh. That equation vastly underestimated the dangers of Hitler and overestimated the strength and ambitions of Ho. It also fed Johnson's comforting belief that American involvement in Vietnam prevented a third world war. Taken together, the exaggerations and illusions so current in Washington in 1963 served for four years to defer a useful official reassessment of the growing American engagement in Vietnam.

As Johnson constantly maintained, Kennedy had raised the stakes. He began in 1961 by ordering 400 Special Force soldiers and 100 military advisers to South Vietnam to provide instruction in counterinsurgency and to organize sabotage in the north. He proceeded to increase the number of American advisers to about 6000 and to assign them missions in conjunction with

Vietnamese troops that resulted in the first American casualties. Though he declined the recommendations of his military advisers to dispatch American bombers and ground troops, his policies forged a "broad commitment" to South Vietnam. At the time of his assassination, he had developed a plan for a gradual withdrawal but was still moving in the opposite direction.

Johnson accepted both that commitment and the assumptions of Kennedy's chief counselors who held that American influence could sufficiently democratize the government of South Vietnam to make it acceptable to the populace, and could infuse the South Vietnam army with the spirit and skills necessary for victory. Those assumptions, ignoring the history and culture of Vietnam, suggested that the United States could buy time by directly assisting the war in the air and on the ground.

So persuaded, Johnson during 1964 moved steadily toward a larger American involvement. In February he ordered the American organization of clandestine strikes against North Vietnam. In May his advisers drafted a congressional resolution authorizing American military action, which the President held back while awaiting a propitious occasion for its introduction. Meanwhile the Joint Chiefs of Staff urged the outright bombing of North Vietnam, a step the draft resolution contemplated. In June Johnson appointed General Maxwell Taylor, an ardent proponent of escalation, as ambassador to Saigon. At the end of July, South Vietnamese commandoes, on a mission Americans had designed, raided two islands in the Gulf of Tonkin. While resisting that invasion, early in August North Vietnamese patrol boats fired on the American destroyer *Maddox*, then engaged in electronic surveillance in the area. Another American destroyer was allegedly attacked two days later.

Now Johnson had his pretext. Claiming the attacks were unprovoked, he ordered retaliatory air raids, earlier planned, against North Vietnam, and he sent his redrafted resolution to the Congress. It authorized the President to take "all necessary measures to repel any armed 'attack against the forces of the United States and to prevent further aggression." The Senate passed the Tonkin Gulf resolution by a vote of 88 to 2, the House, unanimously. Though those majorities reflected in part a response to the administration's calculated deceit, though debate in both houses revealed considerable confusion about the implications of the resolution, though several speakers observed that the authorization did not terminate congressional responsibility for determining national policy or give the president carte blanche, Johnson thereafter interpreted the resolution as tantamount to a declaration of war.

He could not yet admit the possibility of war in Vietnam. In the midst of his campaign for election, he made moderation the theme of his foreign policy. Barry Goldwater's reckless rhetoric about Vietnam helped the President. An open advocate of heavy bombing, Goldwater seemed also prepared to use tactical atomic weapons. Democratic campaign propaganda depicted him as a merchant of death. For his part, Johnson maintained that he was merely carrying out Kennedy's policies, preserving democracy in South Vietnam, and containing Communist aggression in Asia. Only two days after he signed the Gulf of Tonkin resolution, the President, referring indirectly to Goldwater, condemned those "eager to enlarge the conflict" in Vietnam. "They call upon us," he said, "to supply American boys to do the job that Asian boys should do. They ask us to take reckless action which might risk the lives of millions and engulf much of Asia." Throughout the campaign, Johnson also contrasted his purpose with that of those like Goldwater—he did not hint at the views of the Joint Chiefs—who "say that we ought to go north and drop bombs."

Surely Johnson would like to have won in Vietnam without recourse to American bombs and troops. His genuine hope that he could, clothed his implications that he would. In 1940 Franklin Roosevelt had promised not to send American boys to fight a European war, a promise he soon found he could not keep.

Roosevelt dissembled for what he considered adequate cause. So did Johnson, but his suggestions to the contrary, the United States stood in far less peril in 1964 than it had in 1940. In 1964 Johnson deluded the electorate because, like Wilson in 1916, he deluded himself. Wilson had then wanted to avoid a war with Germany even though he realized an errant U-boat skipper could force him into one. His taut interpretation of international law had left him small room for maneuver. So with Johnson. By identifying the preservation of an independent government in South Vietnam with the future of democracy everywhere, he had made the defense of that government a test of his and of American credibility and power.

The deterioration of the situation in South Vietnam posed that test early in 1965. The South Vietnamese army, its morale low as usual, appeared close to collapse. A new government in Saigon under the military brace of General Nguyen Van Thieu and Air Marshal Nguyen Cao Ky needed American support to survive. No more democratic than their predecessors, Thieu and Ky seemed potentially more efficient. Their prospects, according to Johnson's advisers, depended upon American bombardment of the north in order to break the will of Ho Chi Minh or at least stop the flow of supplies from Hanoi to the Viet Cong, the insurgents in the south. In February a Viet Cong attack resulted in the killing of some American advisers at the base at Pleiku. With that episode as his excuse, Johnson ordered the start of Operation Rolling Thunder, the systematic bombing of northern targets, which with occasional interruptions he was gradually to escalate for many months. By the end of 1968 Americans had dropped 3.2 million tons of bombs on Vietnam, more than they had used in all of World War II.

The Joint Chiefs, while eager for the bombing, had never expected it to suffice. General William C. Westmoreland, in command in Saigon, believed as they did that only American ground troops could buttress the sagging South Vietnamese army. In June 1965 Johnson met most of Westmoreland's request for troops, and by the end of the year 184,000 American soldiers were in Vietnam. Acting on the basis of the Tonkin Gulf resolution and his own authority as commander in chief, Johnson did not consult Congress about sending those men or the thousands who followed them. No other president had ever before dispatched an equivalent army wholly on his own or to so remote a place. In doing so, Johnson stretched his constitutional power to and probably beyond its limits. He put the country into a land war in Asia from which extrication was bound to be extremely difficult. Troops once there needed supplies which the Congress could not readily deny them. Johnson had crossed an ominous threshold; he had Americanized the war.

The Americanization of the war accomplished what earlier policy had portended. Americanization also strengthened the case of senators who had made a career of sponsoring military expenditures useful to their states and constituents. Worse, it wrapped the war in the Star-Spangled Banner. Henceforth dissent could be labeled un-American. Indeed Johnson and some of his closest advisers excoriated even moderate dissenters, traitors in their special vision; "yellow" in the contemptible epithet of one of the President's staff. Americanization especially played into the hands of the Joint Chiefs of Staff, inveterate advocates as they were of ever more force. Johnson, whose private insecurities may have fed his public certitude, again and again granted those requests at least part way. The number of American troops in Vietnam rose—some 385,000 by the end of 1966; over 485,000 by the end of 1967; over 536,000 by the end of 1968. They suffered more and more casualties—over 1000 in 1965; 4000 in 1966; 7000 in 1967; 12,000 in 1968.

Through it all Johnson remained fastened to the premises that had led him into Vietnam and still led him on. He continued to believe a Communist triumph there would threaten the security of the United States, to identify North Vietnam with China, to think a settlement short of victory would indicate a failure of American will and bring on World War III, to fear that an accommodation in Saigon that included Viet Cong elements would amount to capitulation. The President did make several attempts to negotiate with Hanoi, a prospect to which he asserted he was always open. But his terms demanded victory. He insisted on maintaining the government in Saigon and on the total withdrawal of North Vietnamese forces from South Vietnam before the departure of the Americans. Hanoi could not accept those conditions without surrendering its objectives or without the agreement of the Viet Cong who would not concede to their hated enemies in Saigon. Further, the process of negotiation continually stalled as Johnson would encourage talks by suspending the bombing of the north briefly, and.then resume the bombing before conversations could get underway.

American bombs, dropped alike on northern targets and on supposed strongholds of the Viet Cong in the south, ruined the country, with napalm burning the villages and chemical defoliants destroying the forests. To "liberate" towns from the Viet Cong, American troops demolished them. To protect rice fields from Communism, Americans flooded them. Official army double-talk made synonyms of save and destroy, and used falsified body counts of enemy dead as measures of victory. Yet the more Americans in the field, the more recruits infiltrated from North Vietnam; the more hamlets ruined, the more Viet Cong rose from the rubble.

Through it all Johnson controlled American policy. He was not the creature of the military who continually urged more escalation than he permitted. Partly he held back because mobilization of the National Guard would have provoked much criticism of the war, partly because the costs of the war were mounting with an alarming rapidity and he wanted to minimize any increase in taxes, partly because he never intended to obliterate

Vietnam, though his decisions were leading that way. He even sustained an impracticable vision of victory followed by the reconstruction of Vietnam through American development, of a Vietnamese Great Society replete with poverty programs and a Mekong River Valley Authority. No more than the military did Johnson's sophisticated advisers make up his mind for him. One, Undersecretary of State George Ball, the house dissenter, consistently opposed operations in Vietnam. Though most of Johnson's counselors backed the President, some of them had private doubts, some cautioned Johnson about the predictably grim consequences of his continuing escalation, some spoke their lines by resigning. In the summer of 1966, the senior member of the White House staff, soon to depart, remarked ruefully to one of Johnson's critics that the President had told him he "didn't give a damn about what any one thought about Vietnam."

So it appeared. Johnson paid no heed to a Defense Department study of September 1966 saying Operation Rolling Thunder "had no measurable effect" on Hanoi's capability in South Vietnam. There was "no firm basis," that study concluded, for determining whether "any feasible level of effort would achieve" the goals of the war in the air. A month later Secretary of Defense Robert McNamara, returning from Saigon, told the President that "pacification," the effort to win hamlets from the Viet Cong, had "gone backward." Johnson was undeterred. In November McNamara questioned the judgment of the Joint Chiefs. There was, he informed Johnson, "no evidence" that more troops, again requested by the military, "would substantially change the situation." Johnson disagreed. The President was obviously in command, answerable, so his actions suggested he believed, to no one.

By that time the war had become Johnson's paramount problem. Official optimism notwithstanding, victory on the President's terms remained as remote as ever. The costs of war were cutting into support for the Great Society, for which Johnson had less and less time. After Republican gains in the elections of 1966, gains attributable largely to the war and the domestic division and difficulties it bred, Johnson could no longer control the House of Representatives, and the Congress began to take an increasingly negative stance on domestic spending. More seriously for him, dissent from the war was expanding. A decade later, Johnson's secretary of state, Dean Rusk, in a self-justifying recollection observed that until 1967 the President had met his important opposition from the "hawks," those demanding ever more bombs and troops. That was an insider's judgment. Johnson and Rusk were more aware of the hawks because they were so contemptuous of the "doves," those opposing the war. By 1966 the devastation in Vietnam and the failure of American policy there had brought J. William Fulbright, chairman of the Senate Foreign Relations Committee, to criticize the administration. Other senators were joining him. They were disturbed, too, by Johnson's indifference to the constitutional authority of Congress to declare war, and by his unwillingness to consult the Senate or even properly to inform it about Vietnam. Waving the Gulf of Tonkin resolution in the face of his critics, Johnson used it as a mandate for his policies, for which, he held, further accountability was needless. He was no more responsible to the public whom his spokesmen misinformed. Indeed excessive security classification made learned criticism of the war difficult, though continued leaks of important data made it possible.

Johnson derided the criticism of the reflective journalists and intellectuals among the doves. Walter Lippmann and George Kennan, wisest of American observers of foreign policy, he condemned as "nervous Nellies." His opponents within the universities were motivated, he believed, by their disdain for the South and its sons. In his opinion the eastern press, especially the increasingly hostile *New York Times*, harbored the same prejudice. All the criticism, according to one senile elder statesman among the hawks, was the work of Jews. In 1966 Senator Robert Kennedy recommended constructing a coalition government in Saigon, with some voice for the Viet Cong, as a necessary step toward peace. Vice-President Humphrey dismissed the proposal as a sell out. Johnson thought Kennedy merely an ambitious opportunist. Indeed he and Rusk tended to see Kennedy's hand behind any dissent within the government. The President responded by displaying public opinion polls showing that most Americans supported the war.

Yet by 1966 the protest movement, escalating along with the war itself, especially affected the colleges where young men and women drew evidence for their case from the writings of French observers expert about Vietnam and from the reporting of American journalists on the scene. More generally the evening television news revealed the horror and futility of the war to the whole country. As usual, Johnson was measuring opinion too much in numbers, too little in its intensity of feeling and conviction.

By 1967 the two powerful protest movements of the decade had converged. Martin Luther King Jr., sensitive to the inroads the war was making on the quest for civil rights, joined the champions of peace. That fall some 200,000 people, their ranks including notable artists and intellectuals, marched on the Pentagon to demonstrate against the war. In 1968, with the end of draft deferments for university students, the earlier teach-ins against the war gave way here and there to furious but senseless destruction of buildings. On city streets crowds of young, middle-class Americans, often with the sympathy of their parents, chanted their venomous verse: "Hey, hey LBJ, how many kids did you kill today?" Thousands burned their draft cards; hundreds fled to Canada or Sweden to escape conscription for a battle they could not condone.

By 1966 the radicals had also merged their causes. A renascent Marxism, divorced from Stalin and married to Freud, attractive particularly to the young, condemned capitalism, the government, and American society for fostering war and poverty alike, and often preached revolution, peaceful or violent. The explosion of frustration among urban blacks that had rocked Watts spread through the cities, in 1966 to Chicago, in 1967 most dramatically to Detroit and Newark, though also elsewhere. The war in Vietnam did not cause those outbreaks, but the preoccupation of Washington with the war compromised the remaining credibility of the Great Society among angry blacks long distrustful of whites and the government.

Among ground troops in Vietnam, many of them black, many others from families of meager means, revolt also emerged. American soldiers in Vietnam fought with the valor of the soldiers of earlier wars, but on the whole they lacked the sense of mission of the doughboys of 1917–18, the sense of necessity of the GIs of 1941–45. No protest at home damaged Westmoreland as much as did the disintegration of morale among hundreds of his troops—"LBJ's hit men" in their own phrase. Escape through the solace of drugs, by desertion, by fragging (the wounding or killing of junior officers) marked the experience of the army, as on occasion did a poisonous rage with which American soldiers slaughtered Vietnamese in captured hamlets where every villager looked to the frazzled conquerors like a homicidal insurgent. All wars brought out the worse in those fighting them; Vietnam exceeded the others.

Before the end of 1967 even the polls were turning against Johnson. Vietnam, as Walter Lippmann observed, had become the most unpopular of American wars. So many Americans were so hostile to the President that he could no longer appear comfortably or even safely in public except on military bases or in some parts of the South. Elsewhere insults, obscenities and threats pursued the President of the United States. Virtually a prisoner in the White House, Johnson was sustained by loyal counselors. Neither sycophants nor knaves, they believed, however unwisely, in their policies and the assumptions that informed them. With their support, Johnson held himself accountable no more to public opinion than to the Congress.

In that pass, with Johnson adamant, and with the techniques of radical protest offending a majority of middle-class and blue-collar Americans, temperate but determined opponents of the war, most of them Democrats but many Republicans, looked to politics to find remedy within the system. The season of Ascutney had arrived. To unseat Johson, his opponents needed a strong candidate of their own. In the fall of 1967 Robert Kennedy, the obvious choice, still hung back. He was not persuaded that anyone could defeat an incumbent president and he was sure an attempt on his part would be written off as self-seeking arrogance. After others had also declined, a relative unknown, Senator Eugene McCarthy of Wisconsin, a Stevenson Democrat, agreed to make the race. He was moved by the appeals of young Americans, by his disgust with the war, perhaps above all by his own humane and poetic conscience. Almost no one thought he had a chance. He had at the outset little money, no organization, only an understated but elegant oratorical style. As his colleagues knew, he would probably have made an impish president, unhappy, awkward, and unpredictable in the office. The Johnson camp did not take him seriously; the Kennedys called him the "wrong Catholic." But as it developed, his courage and eloquence caught the enthusiasm of millions of voters fed up with the war. His organization, never really professional, grew on the energy of dedicated volunteers, mostly middle-class amateurs, thousands of them students or housewives.

Shortly before the first primary contest in New Hampshire, McCarthy, then still without a national reputation or following, gained an indispensable boost from an unexpected turn in the war. At the end of January 1968, during the Tet holiday—the Vietnamese lunar New Year—a surprise attack threw back American and South Vietnamese forces in the provincial capitals and even threatened the American embassy in Saigon. The gains were temporary, bought at the cost of casualties so heavy that the American command claimed a victory. Confidentially, however, Westmoreland asked for another 200,000 troops and the Joint Chiefs recommended a call-up of the reserves. In that light the claims of victory struck a sour note. The public knew at least that the administration had asserted at the beginning of the year that the enemy was near collapse. Instead the enemy had mounted a dramatic offensive. Johnson's already shaky credibility fell further, as did his popularity.

In March in New Hampshire McCarthy polled 42.5 percent of the vote to the President's 49.5. Almost anonymous four months earlier, the senator had almost outstripped the President. Days later, now certain Johnson could be beaten, long dubious about McCarthy, Kennedy entered the race. "I run," he announced, "to seek new policies—policies to end the bloodshed in Vietnam and in the cities, policies to close the gap between black and white, rich and poor, young and old." Kennedy, as Johnson knew, had access to funds and a professional organization, as well as the confidence of the poor, the blacks, and the "ethnics"—the third generation descendants of the foreign born. The polls already showed him equal in strength to Johnson among Democrats and independents. McCarthy would certainly go on to win in the primary in Wisconsin; before the Democratic convention, Kennedy would probably prevail.

To the astonishment of the American people, on the night of March 31, 1968, the President announced that he would not campaign for renomination. He withdrew, he said, in order to end the divisiveness in the country and to concentrate on ending the war in Vietnam. To spur negotiations with Hanoi, he was calling a partial halt to the bombing. His critics, then and later, ascribed his decision to fear of defeat. Lyndon Johnson hated defeat as much as he hated Kennedy, and it had never been his temperament to run from a tough fight. Indeed he continued to fight for control of his party, though now in behalf of the candidacy of Vice-President Humphrey. Johnson still intended to win.

Granted his own explanation, the President had resolved to make a last, honest effort to salvage both his reputation and his purpose. So long as he was himself a candidate, he realized, his opponents would suspect his motives. Further, terms for peace in Vietnam could no longer remain unconditional. The loss of lives there and of tranquility at home had always depressed him. Now Westmoreland's request for more troops focused his choice. Johnson had jiggled Robert McNamara out of office because of his hesitations about the war, but by March many of his other, most trusted advisers, longtime hawks, were urging him to move to end the conflict. So spoke Johnson's old friend and new secretary of defense, Clark Clifford; so also former secretary of state Dean Acheson, senior cold warrior in Washington, and the other "wise men," experienced American statesmen, whom the President summoned for consultation toward the end of March. It was their council and his own similar instinct that finally persuaded the President to alter course.

Frustration, bitterness, and tragedy imbued the rest of Johnson's term. North Vietnam quickly agreed to negotiate, but there ensued long wrangling over conditions for discussion, and President Thieu of South Vietnam asserted his stubborn insistence on excluding representatives of the National Liberation Front, the Viet Cong's political arm, whose presence Hanoi demanded. For six months talks led nowhere while the fighting continued. Making peace was proving as difficult as making war. Earlier Johnson had reluctantly proposed a surtax on incomes, which Congress had delayed enacting. It was in any case too little, too late to arrest the grave deterioration in the American balance of payments or the debilitating onset of inflation, both of which were to continue for years to the damage of the Great Society programs. The course of politics signaled the repudiation of Johnson. Humphrey, once a liberal hero, now carried the burden of his own identification with the President and the war. His candidacy paled as McCarthy held the affection of his middle-class adherents and Kennedy made stunning gains among the poor and the minorities, while also attracting a corps of Democratic chieftains eager for party victory. In April the terrible assassination of Martin Luther King Jr., distressed the nation and set off riots in the black ghettoes. Kennedy appeared to be the only leader who could heal the country. Then in June, the night of his victory in the California primary, Kennedy, too, was murdered. The millions who mourned him grieved also for his creative liberalism. To some the country seemed so sick that all the brave young men must die.

At the Democratic convention in August Humphrey easily won nomination on the first ballot. He inherited a shattered party. So despised was the President that he had not dared to attend. His dominating regulars bulled through an implausible platform which sang praise for his achievements. They mocked and bullied the McCarthy delegates. Worse, the Chicago police, angry as were so many blue-collar Americans with the antiwar demonstrators who had flocked to the city to witness for peace, engaged in a saturnalia of brutality. Shouting "Kill, kill, kill," the police clubbed thousands of demonstrators and spectators, even cameramen trying to film the outrage which nevertheless reached national television, as did the raucous meanness of the convention's masters. What had been the party of the New Deal, the party of reform, seemed in that disheartening picture the party of repression and revenge.

Even with Richard M. Nixon as his Republican opponent, Humphrey could not rebuild fast enough. He tried. The unions brought many of their members into his fold. Other Democrats returned simply because they could not abide Nixon. Humphrey also attempted gently to dissociate himself from the war and the continuing bombing. To assist that effort, Johnson suspended all bombing on October 31, but Thieu still blocked negotiations, sure that a Republican president would soon improve his chances. Alabama Governor George Wallace, running on a third-party ticket, drew off enough southern segregationist and northern working class votes to hurt Humphrey and give the election, by a slim margin, to Nixon, an inveterate hawk whose promise by unspecified means to bring peace to Southeast Asia was worth no more than his promises had ever been.

A fractured party, the remnants of a progressive program about to be scuttled, a continuing and unpopular war, the wretched Nixon—those were parts of Johnson's legacy to his country. He tried to bequeath illusion, too. "We had . . . defeated aggression," Johnson wrote in his memoir. ". . . We had given 17 million South Vietnamese a chance to build their own country . . . and . . . seen them move well down that road." He blamed his setbacks on the communists, the intellectuals, the Kennedys. "Deep down," he said, "I knew . . . that the American people loved me." After all he had done for them, he asked, how could they help but love him; "I was sabotaged." Alas, there were those around him who shared that sad fantasy.

It was especially sad because Johnson, who had accomplished so much, managed the destruction of his own hopes. He was not entirely at fault. He attacked the poverty and the discrimination he found around him. He inherited the assumptions of the cold war and the conflict in Vietnam, though he did not question them. A giant of a kind, he writ large the problems of the presidency and the uncertainties of reform. As his own most trusted expert, he could not in the end reconcile his will to the changing temper of the people. Like other liberals before him, he could not understand the place of radical dissent. But it was his own temperament that associated any criticism with prejudice, cowardice or treachery. He was without humility, unaware of irony. It was his warped sense of his own majesty that made him deny his accountability. It was his own naked and shivering nature that demanded all the credit for his victories and declined any of the blame for his defeats. Lyndon Johnson was a force, but his mass and velocity left ruin in the wake of his heady striving.

Epilogue: Past Imperfect

By 1966 the American presidency had become the most powerful office in the world. The strength of the nation had made that eminence possible; the progressive presidents had made it actual. They did so while using their office to sponsor necessary social and economic reforms and to manage demanding international affairs. Without exception, they believed in active federal government and a strong chief executive. By and large American liberals agreed with them, though with rising anxiety about the possibility of presidential autocracy that inhered in Lyndon Johnson's manner of governing.

In 1968 that concern and others attended Johnson's nomination of Abe Fortas as chief justice of the United States. A vintage New Dealer, Fortas had notable talents as a lawyer and had served admirably as an associate justice of the Supreme Court. Also an old friend and adviser of Johnson, he had consistently supported the war in Vietnam. Now the Republicans aimed to reserve the appointment of a new chief justice for Nixon. Southern conservatives, distressed by the court's advocacy of civil rights, considered Fortas another undesirable liberal. Some antiwar liberals wanted to punish Johnson. The resulting coalition blocked approval of Fortas. He had been overeager, perhaps, in seeking lucrative speaking engagements, indiscreet in driving a Rolls Royce. But he was not corrupt, nor was he the first distinguished justice to advise a president. The Senate blocked Fortas largely because Johnson's critics had found his presidency too powerful. "The Presidency," a perceptive scholar wrote in 1966, "has absorbed the Cabinet, the Executive departments, the Vice-Presidency. It has taken over the national party apparatus. . . . It has a powerful influence on the doctrine of the Supreme Court. It has transformed the federal system. . . . As a responsible opposition to the President, Congress is almost a total failure." That assessment indicated the revolution that had taken place in the office since Woodrow Wilson's contempt for it in 1885.

The reaction to Lyndon Johnson initiated a reconsideration of all the progressive presidents whose administrations appeared to their critics to raise the very issues over which Johnson had stumbled. So it was that the American right again railed against the dangers of federal power. Government regulation of private enterprise, in that conception, ripped apart an indivisible fabric of freedom that included individual rights. Spokesmen of the right seemed to argue that the progressive presidents and their adherents had invented false issues in order to aggrandize government and themselves. In contrast, the young Marxists of the New Left maintained that a capitalist state inevitably created repressive conditions. In that analysis, moderate reform served corporate interests as certainly as did outright indulgences to private wealth. The progressive presidents, in that light, had been disingenuous agents of corporate capitalism. For their part, liberal intellectuals, scorned alike by the right and the left, recognized that Johnson's behavior had called into question their traditional faith in a strong president as the appropriate instrument of social reform.

The continuing ambiguities of American liberalism provided some explanation for each of those views, yet each also overlooked as much as it comprehended. The rightists were the prisoners of a stroboscopic nostalgia for a time that had never been. Neither the federal government nor the presidents invented the problems they had tried to solve. Rather, Theodore Roosevelt and his successors recognized that special interests, particularly corporate interests, had accumulated a decisive power in American society for which they were responsible to no authority, a power they exercised without regard for its consequences in poverty and injustice. Only the federal government could counterbalance that power. That government was accountable to the whole people and could be made more so by the democratization of election practices, which the progressives urged. Within the federal government, the courts had condoned and the Congress had failed to remedy the inequities in American society and the discontent they bred. Those conditions put it to the president to effectuate the enactment and execution of remedial laws. To regulate business, to subsidize desirable social and economic activities beyond the intention or scope of private enterprise, to redistribute income, eventually to moderate the business cycle, the federal government had to grow, as it did especially under Franklin Roosevelt. American liberals welcomed that growth because their social goals depended upon it. In directing the government in the necessary discharge of its responsibilities, the president had to play a central role, for his leadership was crucial to the process, and his capabilities to lead required an expansion of his staff as

well as of his authority. Theodore Roosevelt defined the office to
those ends; Wilson and Franklin Roosevelt—partly under the
burdens of war—enlarged and refined that definition; Johnson
accepted it as his mandate.

Radical critics of the progressive presidents condemned them
for rejecting socialism, as they did. The state capitalism fostered
by American liberalism, as Marxists asserted, failed to achieve a
just society or a peaceful world. Like most of their constituents,
the presidents gave too little thought to the inadequacies of the
American system. But no system produced universal charity and
equality, and socialist states, disinclined to question the essentials
of their own system, did not abjure repression at home or aggression abroad. Even if the United States might have gained from
the revolution the radicals recommended, the vast majority of the
American people thought otherwise. The progressive presidents,
all of them opposed to radical change, did not prevent dissent,
though they sometimes tried to. Rather, that dissent failed to
convince any significant number of Americans that, in spite of
their discontents, they would benefit from revolution.

The radicals failed to persuade partly because the progressive
presidents accomplished as much as they did. Gradualism in the
cause of reform had imposing cumulative effects, though large
problems remained only partly solved. Federal authority did not
reach significiant parts of the private sector. There was no responsible check on the informal alliance between industry and the
military. Endeavor though it did to help the poor by taxing the
rich, the government did not much alter the early twentieth-cen-
tury pattern of the distribution of wealth, though the volume of
wealth multiplied. Those shortcomings arose not from a lapse in
liberal purpose but from the persistence of conservative strength.
Gradualism worked both ways. The progressive presidents succeeded in continual increments to advance the nation toward
their goals, but conservative presidents and conservative congresses ordered continual retreats. Even so the progressives did

enough to sustain the American system by improving it. Their essential conservatism saved the country from a cosmetic conservatism, an adherence to the status quo, which, had it prevailed continuously after 1900, would have spawned the radicalism that liberals disclaimed.

The progressive presidents did not make the United States a world power. The nation had become one by 1900. The president could not ignore the consequences of its international station, for the Constitution made him head of state and commander in chief. Theodore Roosevelt and his successors, comfortable with their authority over domestic affairs, exercised it more broadly in world affairs. In making foreign policy, especially in times of war, they extended their power to and sometimes beyond its elastic constitutional limits. Though Congress lacked the ability or coherence to make foreign policy, it retained the authority to check the president's decisions. None of the progressive presidents was wholly content with that proper restraint or entirely ingenuous in working within it. Still, none created the international tensions with which he had to cope. They could not permit the United States to play the role of a passive observer in an unruly world because the impact of world conditions precluded passivity. The presidents erred most grievously when the course of world politics or the prosecution of war persuaded them arbitrarily to invade the legitimate rights of other nations or the individual rights of Americans. The emergency of war also moved them to subordinate important domestic objectives to the priority of speedy victory. Those occasions did not grow out of liberal doctrine but out of the fallibility even of responsible men. Yet the occasional excesses of the progressive presidents in their conduct of foreign policy and war served as timely reminders of the need for accountability in all exercises of power.

To that end the Constitution imposed its celebrated checks, which narrowly interpreted, militated against the exercise of any useful authority at all. That interpretation did not serve, for without a strong president, government floundered. So it was in the last decades of the nineteenth century, so again in the 1920's, the 1950's, and the latter years of the 1970's. Active presidents, active leaders trained and eager to lead, served as catalysts for creative change. Yet the power they gladly accumulated had to be held responsible to the law and to the people. The preservation of that balance required a nice combination of vigilance and restraint in the Congress, in the courts, and among an electorate prepared to organize to express its will. So, too, it required a president accepting of his accountability—not supine, not timid in the face of rigid legal doctrine or selfish congressional obduracy, not ruled by the polls or fooled by them, conscious of the limits of his office while prepared to press against them, aware of the need to learn and to deliberate as well as to preach and to act; a president adept in politics but not consumed by them, a president as ready to face the nation as to lead it. Neither constitutional stipulations nor historical precedents guaranteed that equilibrium of power and of person. Predictably the progressive presidents wrote imperfect chapters in the record of the past. The conditions and accidents of their times called the four men forth, though others like them would have done as well. In spite of their limitations, their positive achievements promoted the general welfare, one stated purpose of the Constitution. In spite of the common ambiguities with which they lived, they provided a vibrant direction that in the large raised the quality of national life.

Notes on Reading

MY OBLIGATIONS to other historians exceed by far the scope of this note. I have profited from their works not only in the preparation of this one but also in writing four other books, mentioned below, in which I have explained my major debts. I owe special thanks to three friends who have over the years generously shared their views with me—though not about this book—without in the least bearing any responsibility for my own: Arthur M. Schlesinger, Jr. and Elting E. Morison, with both of whom I have on occasion collaborated, and Kingman Brewster whose ideas about power and accountability I have borrowed with reward. What follows is a list of the studies on which I have drawn most heavily for this book, all of them also of potential interest for readers who would like to explore further some of the subjects here discussed.

Of the whole library of general works on the presidency, those that especially helped me in thinking about this analysis were J. M. Burns, *Presidential Government* (Boston, 1966), M. Cunliffe, *American Presidents and the Presidency* (2nd edition, New York, 1976), G. E. Reedy, *The Twilight of the Presidency*, (New York, 1970), and particularly A. M. Schlesinger, Jr., *The Imperial Presidency* (Boston, 1973).

On Theodore Roosevelt and his administration, I relied particularly on my own study, *The Republican Roosevelt* (2nd edition, Cambridge, 1977), but also on the insights of E. E. Morison, the editor of *The Letters of Theodore Roosevelt*, 8 v. (Cambridge, 1951–1954), and the author of a splendid biography of Henry L. Stimson, *Turmoil and Tradition* (Boston, 1960), as well as the stunning essay, from which I have quoted liberally, "Theodore Roosevelt Appoints a Judge," *Massachusetts Historical Society Proceedings*, LXXII, 309–322. A. M. Paul in his *Conservative Crisis and the Rule of Law* (Ithaca, 1960) provides a telling analysis of the views of the Supreme Court at the turn of this century. In two books, *The Triumph of Conservatism* (Glencoe, 1963) and *Railroads and Regulation* (Princeton, 1965), G. Kolko puts forward his interpretation of progressive legislation as a victory for business interests, a contention skillfully challenged in the case of meat-packing by J. Braeman in *Albert J. Beveridge* (Chicago, 1971). There is a recent, informed and critical assessment of Roosevelt's presidency in L. L. Gould, *Reform and Regulation: American Politics, 1900–1916* (New York, 1978).

The most eminent of Wilson scholars, A. S. Link, has published five volumes of biography indispensable for any account of Wilson's administration: *Woodrow Wilson*, 5 v. (Princeton, 1947–1965). I benefited, too, from reading G. Levin, *Woodrow Wilson and World Politics* (New York, 1968). I have not wholly agreed with either author in this book or in my *Woodrow Wilson and the Politics of Morality* (Boston, 1956).

The fullest and liveliest study of Franklin D. Roosevelt's first administration is in A. M. Schlesinger, Jr., *The Coming of the New Deal* (Boston, 1959) and his *The Politics of Upheaval* (Boston, 1960). Also of the first importance are W. E. Leuchtenburg, *Franklin D. Roosevelt and the New Deal* (New York, 1963), which carries the narrative to 1940, and J. M. Burns, *Roosevelt: The Lion and the Fox* (New York, 1956) and *Roosevelt: The Soldier of Freedom* (New York, 1970). My disagreements, such as they are, with those authors derive from my analyses in two books of my own, *Roosevelt and Morgenthau* (Boston, 1970) and *V Was For Victory* (New York, 1976), as well as from the ideas presented in E. W. Hawley, *The New Deal and the Problem of Monopoly* (Princeton, 1966), and R. Lekachman, *The Age of Keynes* (New York, 1966). An excellent recent study, R. Dalleck, *Franklin D. Roosevelt and American Foreign Policy, 1933–1945* (New York, 1979), encapsulates and enhances much of the best of earlier research and writing on that subject.

In dealing with Lyndon Johnson, I depended entirely on the publications of others, for I have examined none of the archives or personal papers relating to Johnson's administration. Since I had a close familiarity with the records of the three other presidents this book discusses, I felt particularly tentative in Johnson's case. That tentativeness, of which readers of this book should be aware, grew also out of my uneasiness with Johnson's memoir, *The Vantage Point* (New York, 1971). It is worse than disappointing. Though Johnson signed it, he obviously did not write it, and those who did lost the flavor of his rhetoric and a commitment to the truth. The book aims to provide instant and total vindication for everything Johnson did. It presents a flat, distorted, and often almost paranoid account of his presidency. The narrative as it relates to Vietnam fails much of the time to correlate with the more reliable data in *The New York Times'* publication of *The Pentagon Papers* (New York, 1971). Still, The *Vantage Point* is worth reading because of what it says in spite of itself about L B J. There is some special pleading in even the most rewarding studies of the Johnson years. Some of the more revealing of those are T. Hoopes, *The Limits of Intervention* (New York, 1968); E. F. Goldman, *The Tragedy of Lyndon Johnson* (New York, 1969); and particularly the sympathetic D. Kearns, *Lyndon Johnson and the American Dream* (New York, 1976), as well as her supplementary essay in *The New Republic*, March 3, 1979. There is little sympathy in R. Evans and R. Novak, *Lyndon B. Johnson: The Exercise of Power* (New York, 1966). A vivid but inaccurate and biased analysis is D. Halberstam, *The Best and the Brightest* (New York, 1972). In *Robert Kennedy and His Times* (Boston, 1978), A. M. Schlesinger, Jr. leans unabashedly toward his subject but nevertheless has much to say about Johnson that is shrewd, indeed indispensable.

Index